DOING TIME ON PLANET EARTH

Adrian Duncan first came into contact with astrology in India in 1970. He is now a full-time professional astrologer practising in Denmark where he is establishing a school for astrologers. He is the Chairman of *Ekliptika*, the astrological association in Copenhagen and has been running courses and lectures in England, Canada, America, Holland, France, Norway and Denmark since 1981.

Doing Time on Planet Earth

ADRIAN DUNCAN

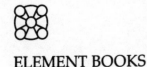

ELEMENT BOOKS

First published in Great Britain in 1990 by
Element Books Limited
Longmead, Shaftesbury, Dorset

Series editor: Steve Eddy
Cover illustration by Peter Irvine
Cover design by Max Fairbrother
Designed by Roger Lightfoot
Typeset by Selectmove Ltd, London
Printed and bound in Great Britain by
Billings Ltd, Hylton Road, Worcester

British Library Cataloguing in Publication Data
Duncan, Adrian
   Doing time on planet Earth.
   1. Astrology
   I. Title
   133.5

ISBN 1-85230-190-2

To my son Tommy, whose Aquarian birth in India in 1971 awoke the consciousness of a New Age in me. To my second son James for his calm wisdom. To the people of India and my present-day teachers – amongst whom I gratefully acknowledge my clients over the last ten years. And above all to my wife Nini, whose wholehearted support and practical help have been invaluable.

Adrian Duncan,
Copenhagen, June 1990

Contents

Foreword

Towards an Integral Astrology

The concept of an integral astrology – meaning an astrology which is genuinely whole or complete – was central to the work of the late, great John Addey, one of the towering figures of twentieth-century astrology. In Addey's holistic utopia the ideal astrologer would be versed in the philosophical and spiritual nuances of both ancient and contemporary cosmology while being competent to conduct scientific research in the mode of the modern materialists. She, or (less frequently, for most astrologers are women) he, would be schooled in the traditions of Claudius Ptolemy or Guido Bonatus yet equally at home with the modern disciplines of astrological therapy and counselling.

It is a fact of life in the twentieth century that many astrologers, while paying lip-service to holism, turn away from any hope of fulfilling Addey's dream and instead confine themselves to their chosen specialities. It is therefore a delight to be asked to write the foreword to a book which promotes a true integral astrology and which does so in such a witty and accessible style.

Adrian Duncan is a practising astrologer, and the bulk of the material he presents is based directly on his experience of working with clients. He writes as a virtuoso, superficially adopting a modern televisual style, filled with sound bites and eye-catching images, yet all the while he leads us deeper into a realm of profound mystery and understanding. Duncan's jocular style lulls the reader into a sense of security, leaving her – or him – unaware when the final philosophical *coup de grâce* is delivered. I am reminded of nothing so much as the games Zen masters play with their students.

Like any experienced Zen teacher, Duncan is a pragmatist. Astrology is to him not so much a matter of the Truth, as a model which enables us to make sense of our place in the cosmos. It is but one model, one path to understanding, and within the whole there are many sub-models. The astrologer may turn from one to the other, moving from science to psychology to divination, and within astrology, between nativities, horaries and mundane cycles, drawing from traditional teachings and modern practice with flexibility and understanding, and always on the basis of what is useful in the moment.

I am especially pleased to see Duncan's revival of the consultation chart, set either for the moment the client arranges the consultation or arrives at the astrologer's consulting room. These are the moments at which the relationship between client and astrologer is sealed in the heavens, and my own experience of such charts has always been that they are invaluable guides to the client's general state of mind. This is not surprising, for they are transit horoscopes, indicating those issues which are of most immediate personal importance. I have found, for example, that the most powerful planetary aspects at the time when astrologer and client meet, especially those from outer planets to angles, invariably point to the questions which the client is waiting for the astrologer to articulate or answer.

These practices raise various radical questions. For example, we may consider the proposition that the astrologer is subsumed within the consultation chart together with the client, thus becoming an equal participant in the consultation or counselling exercise, sharing in a joint dialogue with destiny. What does this suggest about the role of the astrologer, her or his ability to manipulate the situation, projection onto the astrologer by the client, and the host of other psychological complexities which litter the astrologer's practical business? The controversial

and slightly disturbing question is raised as to whether
the conduct and outcome of the consultation, an exercise
designed to enhance freedom of choice, is itself fated. Such
paradoxes are grist to Duncan's mill, for he understands
that astrology has flourished within our dualistic model
of the universe, where matter is pitted against spirit, good
against evil and so on. Astrology is a universal language
– the language of time – allowing people from different
cultures to build bridges and communicate, yet it also
stands at the interface of different dimensions, specifically
time and space. Indeed, it's the meeting of time and space
which gives astrology its unique nature.

Our models of astrology change with time, adapting to
an evolving human environment. For example, modern
technological innovations challenge our former practices;
what effect, Duncan asks, will digital clocks have upon
our appreciation of time? Many astrologers see only bad
in the digitalisation of time, fearing that it will finally
destroy the cyclical notion of time perpetuated by the
traditional clock face. But Duncan is an optimist, refuting
the Luddites and suggesting that digital clocks both return
us to Pythagorean and Platonic truths by reaffirming
the primary importance of number, and encourage the
perception of astrology as omen divination by replacing
reliance on the phase of the cycle by attention to the magic
of the moment. He doesn't claim that any one mode of
these competing modes of perception is superior, only that
each is valid in its own way and has its own application.

An amusing instance of technological interference in the
astrological process is provided by the fictitious example
of a horary astrologer on a trans-Atlantic jet, casting a
horoscope for one of his fellow passengers. The problem
here, of course is one of rapidly changing coordinates
as the astrologer hurtles not just through time but also
space. For which location is the horoscope to be set? Few
of us may be in this situation, but the question remains
– what *will* the astrologers of the next century do when
faced with horoscopes cast for the Moon or even for some
interplanetary craft?

In a sense Duncan's perspective is sociological: astrological models are relative, evolving as part of broader cultural change. So, for example, contemporary developments in astrological thought and practice may be prompted by modern digital clocks and jet travel. On the other hand, time is itself an expression of consciousness, while cultural history itself takes place within the longerterm astrological cycles of the outer planets and fixed stars. Duncan therefore hints at the existence of two levels of astrology. On the one hand there is a Truth with a capital T, represented in the unfolding consciousness of the universe as witnessed through the precession of the equinoxes, the Jupiter–Saturn mutations and similar cycles. On the other there are truths, with small t's, as embodied in our evolving models of the cosmos and the rules we construct for interpreting planetary symbols and reading horoscopes. By this means we grope our way to an understanding of the greater Truth. The general shift in modern astrological practice from event-orientated prediction towards psychologically based counselling therefore represents a move from one truth to another. Neither form of astrology is better than the other. Both fulfil needs and are located within different cultures at different times. The greater Truth, meanwhile, remains the same.

In Duncan's view the astrological practice of the past two thousand years, with its incredible variety of truths, corresponds to the superior Truth embodied in the Age of Pisces, while for the coming two millennia of the Aquarian Age, an Aquarian astrology may be preferable. His goal is to lay the foundations for such an astrology which we may define as democratic, compassionate, humanistic, iconoclastic, practical and freed from dogma. Aquarian astrology spans all truths, so keeping open every available avenue by which we may glimpse the Truth. Astrology is not an icon to be worshipped but a means to an end, that end being human happiness. Astrologers themselves are not a new priesthood with exclusive access to higher knowledge but professionals whose task is to listen to their clients and help them. Such an attitude requires care, consideration and humility on the part of the astrologer.

One of the most welcome sections of the book is that where Duncan deals gently with the pitfalls, problems and perils of practising as a professional astrologer. His case-notes offer valuable insights into the vexed question of what to actually *do*, let alone *say*, when the client arrives. I'd recommend this section both to every beginner contemplating setting up a practice and to teachers who skirt around the delicate issue of what will happen when their students are at last unleashed on the public.

As a historian I appreciate Duncan's willingness to locate his radical approach, with its multiplicity of high-tech images and lateral connections, in astrological tradition. For example, he correctly points out that the horary figures that form the core of most surviving medieval and Renaissance case-notes were in fact consultation charts and that it was these, rather than nativities, which formed the backbone of astrology until the seventeenth century. The modern vogue for natal astrology, which is often attributed to the superior individuation and consciousness of twentieth-century people, may be better ascribed to political developments – the spread of centralised bureaucracies requiring the recording of birth times in order to facilitate social control – combined with technological inventions – the perfection of the mechanical clock. When both these innovations were in place birth times could be kept and natal horoscopes cast. In his delightful way Duncan therefore manages to put the record straight with a down-to-earth view of why modern astrology has assumed its current models and priorities.

Duncan's title, *Doing Time on Planet Earth*, apparently a slick use of the idiom for going to prison, takes us deeper into our philosophical past: common amongst the gnostic and hermetic astrologers of the time of Christ was a belief that the physical world was a prison in which the free soul was incarcerated, hemmed in by the planets, themselves representing the bars on the prison window. Beyond the bars lay heaven, the realm of peace and perfection, to which the soul would eventually return. The gnostic or hermetic astrologer was prone to resent the planets for obscuring his view of heaven, whereas Duncan, while evoking the image of the cosmos as prison, has replaced hermetic gloom and gnostic despair with a jocular attitude of 'it's not really so bad, and while we're here we might as well enjoy ourselves'!

In Duncan's *laissez-faire* model of the universe, fate and free will are no longer enemies to be set at each other's throats or contradictory concepts to be agonised over, as they have been in the dualistic Age of Pisces but, in line with the intellectual versatility of the Aquarian principle, equally useful models of existence, each of which has its own place. Acceptance of fate, he muses, makes us feel better about the past, while belief in free will enables us to face the future. In other words, life can only get better! One is almost tempted to quote Bob Dylan – 'Ah, but I was so much older then, I'm younger than that now'; the body may age but the psyche gets younger.

This book is written for astrologers who are young at heart – who will relish its iconoclastically modern approach – and those who are not – who will be challenged to change their ideas. It's less another astrology book, more a remarkable personal statement from a self-proclaimed lateral thinker.

Nicholas Campion,
April 1990

'The Astrodial'

Introduction

Welcome to an exercise in lateral thinking. This is the world of Uranus, on whose lateral landscape the astrologer roams. Here we see interconnections between iron, the sword, anger, energy and drive, war and the planet Mars; between frustrated love, the stock market, the businessman, emotional isolation and Venus–Saturn combinations.

Sceptics will throw their hands up in the air, for this book is not an attempt to explain or justify astrology, which has been part of my everyday life for so long, and has enriched it immeasurably. On the contrary, it is a celebration of the subtle and all-encompassing interplay between man and the cosmos, reflected in everyday life.

Statisticians will nod with an air of satisfaction, knowing that nothing in this book can be proved, based as it is on unsubstantiated statements and unscientific intuitions. This book is not going to cause a stir in scientific conferences.

I wish only to introduce my personal experience of reality, hoping that the many ideas presented will strike a chord of recognition in the hearts of readers, so that it will enrich their reality. Students of astrology have often had to answer the question 'How can people on earth be affected by anything as far away as the planets?' Yet we can scent a change in the air. This question is becoming unfashionable; sceptics are beginning to tread more carefully. Modern scientific theory has taken the edge off the sweeping sword of 'scientific respectability'. Nuclear physics is a double-edged sword in which the head of the observer himself is called into question. Now the astrologer can confidently respond: 'How can you possibly believe that the earth and its inhabitants are *not* affected by its intimate integration into the solar system?'

Astrology has its dangers and its pitfalls, and astrologers (myself included) spend a good deal of their time blundering into them. The question of fate versus free will looms quickly up on the horizon. The tendency to use astrological rationalisations can take over, ossifying and amputating the true magic of reality – as all rationalisation systems do. It is hardly appropriate for example to respond to a declaration of love from one's partner with some intellectual comment about mutual astrological aspects.

Many of these faults are not inherent in astrology, but in the Western tradition of thought which does not know how to integrate opposites, and tends to see most issues as black or white. This is the heritage of the Piscean Age, which is now fast losing ground to a new encroaching consciousness under whose neon glare opposites are resolved.

All attempts to systematise knowledge have their drawbacks. The advantage of astrology is that there is virtually no area where it cannot be applied. Different psychological systems draw on the personality of their founders, and are limited by this factor. Astrology is flexible enough to incorporate any thought pattern, and it uses an archetypal symbology which can be applied to the deepest and most esoteric truths, as well as supposedly banal daily events. In this book I wish to make no distinctions between high 'spiritual' realities, and mundane happenings. I haven't noticed that there is any difference.

Acknowledgement

The charts in this book appear courtesy of Electric Ephemeris.

1

A New Face of Time

After three thousand years of explosion, by means of fragmentary and mechanical technologies, the Western world is imploding. During the mechanical ages we had extended our bodies in space. Today, after more than a century of electric technology, we have extended our central nervous system itself in a global embrace, abolishing both space and time as far as our planet is concerned. Rapidly, we approach the final phase of the extensions of man – the technological stimulation of consciousness, when the creative process of knowing will be collectively and corporately extended to the whole of human society. *Understanding Media* – Marshal McLuhan

Year 2000 on the Space/Time Continuum

Let us imagine that the Earth is visited by a space traveller. Having travelled from a distant galaxy in a state of hibernation for countless years, she finally sets foot on our planet, her ship surrounded by curious Earthpeople. Perhaps the first question our traveller will ask is – 'What's the time?'

A self-possessed Earthperson would glance at his quartz watch and promptly say, 'It's 15.39' – hopefully not confusing our galactic guest with old-fashioned a.m. and p.m.

The Space Creature retires to her ship to consult her computer. Perhaps glancing at Sol, the nearest star, she will conclude that she has landed on a planet revolving on its own axis over a period of 24 units of time, and that the area of the Earth where her ship is parked is now somewhat over half-way through a particular unit of time defined as a day.

Rather irritated at this incomplete data she returns to the group of Earthpeople and pursues her line of questioning: 'Yes, but *when* am I?' Our astute Earthperson may then have the presence of mind to explain further that it is, say, 21 June, and after consulting her computer again the traveller would soon realise that the Earth orbited around the visible star she could see, and that this cycle of time could be measured in units called months (conveniently ticked off by an enormous and alarmingly close moon).

Now with both the time and the day of the month she can orientate herself on an orbiting planet that is part of a larger solar system, but it is still not enough – how is she going to find her position in the immensity of galactic space? Persistent enquiry finally elicits from our patient Earthman a full time description: 15.39 on 21 June in the year AD 2000.

All becomes clear to our time traveller. Her computer announces: 'Welcome to planet Earth, a paradise in the system *Sol*, on a distant tip of the Milky Way galaxy.' The year 2000 will reveal the solar system's relationship to the panorama of the stars – 2,000 years after the man/god Christ ushered in the Age of Pisces, the age of the nobility of the suffering of Earth beings, in harmony with the cosmic rays of the ancient zodiacal symbol of the Fishes, as recorded in galactic annals. In its precessional cycle the Earth has aligned its polar 'wobble' with this particular area of the universe and is now in the dying stages of a transition from one constellation to another as part of a longer 26,000 Great Year cycle of time.

By relating then to these interlocking cycles of time, our traveller can orientate herself in space. She can only orientate herself in space through understanding cycles of time, and actually where she comes from they have forgotten how to make a distinction between the two concepts. They live on the cutting edge of the space/time continuum.

To a lesser extent space/time relativity can also be experienced in modern everyday life. Travelling on a flight from New York to Paris – a journey which took many weeks less than a century ago and now takes under four hours by supersonic jet – the cosmopolitan astrologer is faced with a dilemma. He may wish to cast a horary chart for a question asked by a fellow passenger. But a problem crops up. Normally he is used to being in one place – stationary – seeing time as the only variable. A mere glance at his watch solves this problem. But when he is in *rapid* motion there are two moving variables – time and space – which need to be adjusted constantly.

On the supersonic jet it would be most simple to limit the practice of horary astrology to flights from Paris to New York. In this direction the plane's speed will compensate for the movement of the Earth on its own axis, and the Ascendant and houses will remain relatively constant, whilst in the other direction, adjustment of the space co-ordinate will have to take place with tremendous rapidity. How a similar dilemma will be tackled on twenty-first-century flights to the Moon and Mars is another question altogether. Heliocentric astrologers, who practise a Sun-centred astrology may take heart – a new age awaits.

Time was the most important factor in our last age, and our civilisation showed great ingenuity in measuring it. Space/Time will be the continuum on and through which we will experience the new age, and we are in the middle of this breathtaking transition right now – although for many of us this is an unconscious experience. Through conquering space we have transformed our conception of time: the great speed machine heralded by the discovery of Uranus in 1781 has brought us to the cutting edge of time.

We experience this transition in many ways, and for most of us it is a disorientating process. Our senses are constantly bombarded by stimuli, and in a state of distraction we are driven from one sensation to another. Television is the chief tool in this fragmentation of the mind, and the pioneering force in this medium is advertising. Marketing factors ensure that advertisers use their time with optimal effect. Videos and ads tend to have scenes that last a fraction of a second before we are shuttled off to the next visual impact. Our attention span is now so short that we appear to have lost our powers of concentration. This spells death to the old ways of schooling, the linear processes of logic and – ultimately – the concept of time as a predictable flow from past to future, an idea which basically springs from the technology of a past age.

Media trends in America – where for example sports events are fragmented into 'time-outs' (stopping time) and action replays (going backwards in time) – have had a profound effect on the American mind. Many a European visitor to the States will have noticed the attention of their hosts wandering if they cannot invest each moment of their time with attention-grabbing tactics. This is quite a contrast to ancient methods of dealing with time. In China and Japan before the introduction of the clock, time had been measured for thousands of years by the burning of incense, and sweetened with different aromas for different hours and seasons. Present generations do not even hear the ticking of a clock. Future generations will not even see the clock's hands.

From the Mechanical to the Electronic

The Age of Pisces really got its grip on Western civilisation through the technological development that enabled the continuous flow of time to be translated into the movement of the pendulum. Prior to this, time had been measured by observing the flow of water or sand, or through the passage of the Sun across the sky. The invention of a mechanical device meant that the uninterrupted flow of time was converted into dual movement. This set the scene for the transformation of our concept of time and the later industrialisation of the West. Technology could now reflect the age – for Pisces is the age of polarities, of good and bad, night and day, God and Satan.

Younger readers today may be quite unfamiliar with the phenomenon of the tick-tocking of a mechanical clock, omnipresent for older generations. It is an extraordinary way to represent the passage of time. Circular motion is converted into lateral motion. This dislocation of the continuous stream of time made possible a linear representation of time, which has been very useful for the mechanisation of society. Most machines reflect this conversion of rotary flow into linear motion, or vice versa. By the end of the nineteenth century we saw the extension of this principle on a massive scale as the winds of a new age (Aquarius – air/steam) powered the machines of the old. A study of the mechanisation process shows how steel replaces the sinews of the hand in a series of linear, additive repetitive movements until a finished product results. This process is an exteriorisation of the logical processes of the mind and sequential thought. And these sequential chains of the mind are directly paralleled by the view of time promoted by the mechanical clock.

The pendulum and the wheel formed the backbone of the last age, and together they wove the fabric of time on the loom of the consciousness of mankind. In this way the true nature of time was cleverly concealed. This was a most necessary and excellent contrivance for the Piscean Age – the sign of obscurity, deception and illusion. Without this development civilisation would never have reached the extraordinary fecundity of the present epoch which makes possible the birth of the New Age from within the tortured body of Pisces. This indeed was the averred role of Christ, who set his seal on Pisces, promising not to bring peace, but to bring a sword to create division (polarity) amongst men.

Through the pendulum, polarity was made manifest. Through the wheel, the Age of Pisces was brought to life. Can we conceive of a world without the pendulum and the wheel? Yet in the time of Aquarius, the wheel will exist only as an object of curiosity. Indeed, its demise began when we started throwing it through the air: the frisbee signalled the beginning of our new consciousness based on the air sign Aquarius. When the young generation starts playing with the serious tools of the old, then the days of its technology are numbered.

The wheel is an extension of the foot, and, of course, feet are ruled by Pisces. In the Age of Aquarius, man will take flight, being just as comfortable in the air as the previous age was in the water. There will be no need for the foot, nor its extensions – the wheel, the cog or the ship's propeller. The fantastic mechanical extravagances of Late Pisces will be objects of fascination in museums of the future.

The mechanical cacophony will leave the stage, making way for a new, quiet and graceful technology, based on the sweep of the bird's wing. The building block architecture, based as it is on linear thought, will be swept away by a new elastic architecture of sweeping expanses. The new age is cool, and will use cool technology reflecting mastery of the air.

As the muscular extensions of production-line technology disappear, extensions of the mind and nervous system (electronic robots) are born. These electronic armies, whilst ruthlessly casting hapless workers into the unknown emptiness of leisure time, deliver humanity from servitude and slavery in front of noisy machines. As yet we can scarcely imagine the extent of this all-encompassing electronic liberation.

Liquid Crystal

As we are so well aware, a small object called the silicon chip is busy transforming our civilisation at the present time. Nowhere is this more apparent than with the digital watch, which in a short period of time has made our old clockworks of the past totally redundant. Electronification as a transforming factor comes under the planetary domain of Pluto, though there is reason to believe that the silicon chip has its associations with Chiron, the small planetoid discovered in 1976 – at about the time we started getting chips with everything. Every astrological student is aware of the concept of synchronicity whereby the discovery of a planet is paralleled by corresponding scientific and social change on earth. And I think we all can see that the greatest revolution of our time is the information revolution.

This transformation of information technology can be partially associated with the 127–year conjunction cycle of Uranus and Pluto. These planets last met in 1966 in the sign of Virgo (information/organisation). This phenomenal and previously inconceivable gathering and sorting of detail at electronic speed – this unifying of masses of disassociated detail – also calls to mind the exploded belt of the solar system which contains the asteroids, which have in these years of space exploration been mapped in detail by astronomers. These, and Chiron (which has a special role because of its eccentric orbit which approaches the orbit of the last visible planet Saturn, and the first invisible planet Uranus), can certainly be associated with the sign Virgo. Obviously this sign has been exalted to new heights over the last decades, and it is only fitting that this should be so, as the Pisces–Virgo polarity makes way for the transition into the Aquarius–Leo Age polarity.

With the digital watch, time and accuracy have become the personal province of the most humble inhabitant of this earth. Before the seventies only the rich could afford the kind of watch that was accurate, and even then accuracy to the second could not be guaranteed. A modern child now expects a watch to be accurate to a tenth of a second, with stopwatch function, alarm, etc. Moreover this wonder of modern technology is also extremely cheap. This is the market dynamic of Pluto in the transition to a new age. Electronics mean that products can be produced cheaper, more accurately and more and more miniaturised, and this spells the downfall of capitalism as we know it. Since the availability of information through electronics spells the downfall of Communism, the Capitalist–Communist polarity will no longer exist in the New Age.

So, let us look around at the clocks that now surround us at stations and airports. Instead of the sweep of the hand (covering the linear distance of time) we are more and more often confronted with the dry information of digital time. The old clock was unequivocally divided into two sections of twelve hours – before noon and after noon, the culmination of the Sun on the Midheaven being the dividing day time point, and over the nadir at midnight the dividing night time point. This represented a clear division between night and day, and the polarity of light and dark, with all its religious corollaries in the Age of Pisces. With no way of illuminating the dark without casting fiendish shadows, all the demons of the unconscious were consigned to the night time sphere.

When the electric light banished the shadows of the night, and jet travel made people aware of the relativity of day and night (the Sun is always shining on half of the Earth), the primitive division of time into day and night could no longer truly represent reality. Thus we have been given the 24-hour day in our liquid crystal playground. This of course drastically changes our perception of time. The magic – and the power – of number replaces the sleepy grace of the clock's hands. Digital suddenness replaces dignified movement. The clock face becomes number, picture becomes digit. Do we not dream of swashbuckling spy adventures when we are listening to the radio after midnight, and the digital clock gleams 0.07? Are we not struck when we arrive at a station at 11.11?

As Neptune moved into Capricorn – the sign we most associate with the concept of time – we saw the advent of Liquid Crystal. The monumental building achievements purported to have been made by ancient civilisations like Atlantis with the help of large crystals are mimicked by a new mini-generation who fight galactic wars, annihilate Space Invaders and transcend thereby inner borders of space and time with little LCD screens clutched between podgy fingers. With the transits of Saturn and Uranus through Capricorn in the late eighties and early nineties, many more dramatic changes are to be experienced as we learn to negotiate the time-warp engendered by Neptune. We may miss the panoramic view of time with LCD display, but we are given something new. This is the direct awareness of the *now*, with very little relationship to the past or the future. The digital clock does not show what came before, nor what will come afterwards. Neither is there any leeway; it cannot be 'fast' or 'slow'. There is a relentlessness about digital time, which reflects the electric relentlessness of our neon age.

Sports events are now timed to hundredths of a second as the 'moment' is expanded to infinity. We are now getting closer to the 'true' (for the Aquarian consciousness) nature of time. As speeds get higher, time accuracy becomes essential for navigational systems – even hundredths of a second can make a difference of thousands of miles in space travel.

For the astrologer this is significant, because the astrologer deals with time in a very intimate way. His or her job is to examine the nature of the *now*, and the character of time as reflected in the moment. The astrologer examines a segment of the space/time continuum, at the intersection of consciousness with time. Even a question which comes to the consciousness at any given moment is contained in that space/time cross-section, as every horary practitioner knows. The philosophical implications of this knowledge drive the astrologer to the borders of what is mentally acceptable – but beyond these frontiers lies the magic of the moment and the awareness of the earth as a living organism of sublime intelligence.

Just as the astrologer assumes that events on earth must reflect planetary and stellar combinations, so then it must also be true that a study of earth events – even the most minute and apparently insignificant events that occur around one – will reveal planetary forces. Just as the moment contains the past and casts its shadow on the future, so then a study of the forces of the moment (omens and portents) can actually be used as a living horoscope.

Prediction is not just the province of the astrologer, but of every person who is truly aware of what is going on in any given moment of time.

The Light-Path of the Individual

Time, then, is a relative concept, partly based on the technology at our disposal. It has been measured visually by the sweeping hands of the clock, and auditorily through the bell. Earlier generations quickly learned this first priority of growing up, ticking off the hours with the 'little hand' and the minutes with the 'big hand'. How painful those long minutes were before the end of the lesson at school; how quickly the minutes of play rushed by. The years of our childhood were replete with detailed experience; the years of old age rush past. Life accelerates on our journey from cradle to grave, precious moments rushing by.

The speed of time is relative to the intensity of our consciousness at any given moment.

The time of a child can be likened to the rushing mountain stream – narrow, but lively and fast-flowing, entering the winding plains of maturity and losing identity in the wide ocean, which ultimately claims and absorbs the waters, minerals and silts of the river. Each age of life has its tone, and the passage of time is relative to it. Just as the mad flurry of the hummingbird contains an aeon of existence for this small being, so too does the planet have its tone of time. Civilisation on earth has a lifetime which is long in comparison to our seventy years of experience, short compared to the galaxy.

Mercury has its time – short and speedy, reflecting its mischievous character, Saturn has the dignity of its $29\frac{1}{2}$ year orbit. Each of the various planetary cycles reflects something of its astrological quality through the speed of its cycle. As we are fairly rooted in the earth, normally moving rather slowly, we tend to assume that time is a stable measure, not related to space. But on our transatlantic jet, pocket computer in hand, we cannot afford to indulge in this deception. It simply will not work.

As we move out in consciousness into the universe, simple earthly concepts of time and space do not function anymore. This happens in a limited way on earth. It becomes more relevant to measure distance in time, when time is money! When dealing with astronomical concepts, distance has to be measured as a function of time, and the medium with which we measure this distance/time is *light*. Space is measured by the time it takes light to cover. Thus the Sun's distance is nine minutes from the earth, whereas the nearest star is four light years away.

Light, then, is the medium with which we measure time and distance – and this has important philosophical consequences for the astrologer, as far as the understanding of time – and 'karma' – is concerned. To transcend time – and also our karma – we must become 'one' with the light, and the Sun in our horoscope is a symbol for this light. Indeed Einstein said that the breakthrough which was responsible for the theory of relativity came when he imagined himself travelling on a beam of light. Becoming unified with our Sun – our inner identity – is the major challenge for the individual. This is the process of individuation as Jung (the archetypal Leo) described it. According to the laws of nuclear physics, however, no body can attain the speed of light, because its mass increases in proportion to its velocity, attaining infinite mass at the speed of light. Neither can human consciousness merge with the light as long as there is a gram of ego or unresolved karma. Nobody can take any baggage with them on the road to enlightenment.

Einstein's famous equation ($E=mc^2$) has of course its spiritual corollaries. The squaring of the speed of light creates a space/time continuum (just as the squaring of a line creates an area of space) which can be seen as a view of eternity or as 'enlightenment'. Mass can be seen as an individual's accumulated karma, the fruits of past actions, without which there would be no need to re-incarnate, and Energy as the burning light of universal consciousness.

Light is the medium of time; the Sun is the medium of consciousness. Time is an expression of consciousness – it is a measure of our state of consciousness and it is the medium through which our karma is expressed. Character plus Time equals Fate. Our birth horoscope shows the legacy of the past and the stored-up actions of the past which of necessity affect our character and thereby our fate. Life is the unfoldment of these stored-up events – the meeting with karma. Yet if we live in the moment, karma no longer exists. At one with the flow of time, we are 'enlightened'. We would simply not be aware of karma, meeting every moment as it happened, neither reflecting about the past nor speculating about the future. Living in the moment neutralises karma (c^2 = Energy over mass).

We are all aware of this idea of living in the here-and-now, but there would be no need to read a book if one could maintain this state – books are far too linear! People are predictable because they do not live in the moment, and thereby they live out their meeting with personal karma as reflected by the horoscope. Bringing in the concept of karma to the Western mind can be risky. One of the weaknesses of using the concept of karma in astrology is that there is a tendency to take a 'fated' attitude towards the horoscope. All is predestined, so what can you do? You may encounter then, the person who devotes a secret part of his life to cultivating a love affair which his marriage partner is not 'aware' of. Should his wife later divorce him for unknown reasons, it would not be accurate for this person to assume that this was his 'karma' – a legacy from the past. It may well be because of the recently created karma of the present. The trick is not to create a difficult framework for the future by careless actions in the present.

Neon Wonderland

The major tool for the universal transition of human consciousness is the electric light: a kind of artificial substitute for the real thing. Aquarius is an electric wonderland, a glaring neon world, a playground for a new generation, and a torment for the aging tribes of the age of the Fishes. In the dying gasps of the Age of Pisces we are stranded on an expanse of silicon, unable to adjust to a new element.

Through the electric light we have gained mastery over our old adversary – the night. As neon drives out the shadows from our world, we are able to illuminate the forgotten corners of our minds. The quartz crystal vibrates, plasma explodes on screen, and the tyranny of the pendulum is vanquished. Wheel and pendulum leave the stage, electronic digits take over as Pisces makes way for Aquarius. The infinitesimal speed of digital integration, the million yes/no decisions of the computer per second, these things mean the end of the suffering of Pisces on the cross of polarity, and the end of the concept of good and evil as experienced by tormented human consciousness in its meeting with the 'satanic' forces of the unconscious. The 24–hour day means that we can embrace and integrate our shadows.

The invention of the electric light gave the human race control over night – and over time. But we are only at the beginning of the beginning. With the development of laser light we are using light as a tool, and this will have direct repercussions on our experience of time. These hesitant beginnings foreshadow the use of consciousness as a tool, and this will be one of the major occupations of the minds of the Aquarian Age. The use of laser light, and the parallel development of the use of consciousness as a tool, will effect an almost inconceivable transformation in our consciousness of time, and also the twins of matter and energy.

During the Falklands War the British fleet was shaken to the core by a small French missile – the Exocet – which succeeded in sinking a British ship almost every time one was fired. Defence against this missile was rather crude, consisting of firing an advanced cannon at an enormous rate, putting up a barrage of metal in the hope that the missile would be destroyed. Because of the speed of the missile, there was very little time in which this manoeuvre could succeed. Had a laser cannon existed, so little time would have elapsed between sighting and firing the laser, that the missile would not even have moved its own length before being destroyed.

Hollywood star and ex-president Reagan, inspired by *Rambo* and the spate of space movies in the early eighties, grasped the significance of the laser and envisioned a vast laser defence system in space. Here he was responding to the 'spacy' square between Uranus in Sagittarius (outer space) and Jupiter in Pisces, a combination which certainly gives big dreams – even if they are totally unrealistic. Fortunately Saturn was taking up the rear in Sagittarius, and both Gorbachev and the US Congress did their bit to point out the flaws of Star Wars: realism had the last word.

Quite clearly, the application of laser power, hopefully for more peaceful purposes, will transform our concept of time, just as the telephone and jet travel have done. In this age of instantaneous communication and infor- mation retrieval, concepts of time and space become many-faceted. Whether we like it or not, we will be in the *now*, with updates on the hour. The electronic revolution has led to the exteriorisation of individual consciousness, so that major change on earth can work on a global scale. Only through this massive outer transformation can the inner transformation of human consciousness take place.

2

The Planetary Clock

The memory is fragile and the space of a single life is brief,
passing so quickly that we never get a chance to see the
relationship between events; we cannot gauge the consequences of our acts, and we believe in the fiction of past, present,
and future, but it may also be true that everything happens
simultaneously. *The House of Spirits* – Isabel Allende

Back to the Future

One of the main principles of astrology is that anything
initiated at a particular moment in time will reflect the
planetary energies operative at that moment. This parallels
Jung's concept of synchronicity, with the added advantage
that through following past and future planetary movement we can also comment on events outside of our
immediate sphere of time.

Anybody working with astrology must accept this principle completely – and those who do not will only be able to
use the knowledge that astrology gives them in proportion
to their limited belief in the effect of the planets. In the
same way it is curious to see how students of astrology
often draw planetary symbols very small in the beginning,
reflecting this lack of confidence, and as experience reveals
the effect of the planets the symbols get larger, stronger and
firmer.

Astrology's effectiveness is only limited by the consciousness and experience of the astrologer. I can remember

reading in one very well-known beginner's book about a supposed 'flaw' in the concept that a horary chart can be based on the time a letter is received and opened. The author's argument was that the train may have been delayed, the postman's van may have broken down – ergo, the time when the letter is opened is unpredictable and accidental. This is like saying 'If my mother had not travelled to Birmingham and met my father on the bus, I would never have been born'! Time is the least 'accidental' medium that exists.

There is an important corollary to the principle of astrological synchronicity and that is that events that take place around the astrologer at any given moment of time must also reflect the planetary influences of that moment. This converse law is very interesting when we come to the study of omens and portents, and is something that can be used very practically, for example during the consultation (see Chapter 5). It also means that the most important teacher about the influence of the planets is life itself.

I have personally found that my own weaknesses in interpretation basically stem from the fact that I do not believe enough in what I see in the horoscope, and am instead led astray by the client's subjective view. For example a client could come with a Moon–Saturn conjunction and when questioned about her relationship with her mother, she might say that it was very 'close'. If you believe in the horoscope you can be almost sure that there is or has been a problem here somewhere – it may have been resolved, it may not – but you would be doing your client a disservice if you did not find out what it was – and intelligent enquiry will normally reveal how early conditioning from the mother is affecting present relationships and behaviour. There is nothing wrong with the horoscope – the flaws of astrology lie solely with the practitioner.

The horoscope is a map of a particular intersection of space/time, reflecting the influences of that moment. A birth chart reflects then the stored-up influences of a person's identity or karma. There is no accident about that moment of birth – it represents the best possible circumstances for the further development of the individual. The incarnating soul has chosen exactly the right mother, and exactly the right father – even if the father should 'happen' to leave home when the child is 2, or the mother should be incapacitated through illness.

Understanding this has important therapeutic value. Earlier psychological traditions seem to have laid the emphasis of responsibility for an individual's problems on the actions of the parents. This encourages the negative tendency to blame others for one's fate. In actual fact the responsibility is the individual's alone. Why is it sometimes the case that one child experiences the mother as being cold and rejecting, and the other as warm and easy to talk to? There can of course be many reasons, but one possibility could be that the child as a baby demanded more from the mother and evoked rejection. This would be a typical Moon–Saturn pattern. An exaggerated need for security may have been a heritage from acute disappointment in a previous incarnation, or from problems in pregnancy or in the birth process (although trauma in pregnancy and birth can normally be seen in Pluto aspects). One could imagine that the child was less inclined to let go of the breast, or woke up repeatedly at night demanding the mother. In fact several clients who have Saturn and Pluto aspects to the Moon have informed me that their own mothers have told them that that they felt rejected *by the child* at a very early age. If a client can be encouraged to remember some such pattern of the past, then he or she may be able to see the situation from the parent's point of view.

By giving the client a new objectivity, she may realise how she herself evokes events through her character and karma. Not only that, she may also realise that the people who come into her life give her the opportunity to confront her karma and thereby evolve. Her parents have done her the enormous favour of being around for her incarnation. She has used them – that was their karma.

The horoscope at birth is a map of the past actions of the individual, and as such there is no doubt that one could attempt to explain some things connected with past lives. Very difficult to confirm though! Personally I rarely do it, and then normally only if asked to by the client. There are, however, occasions when it is valuable – and this is often with people who have many planets in Scorpio, strong Pluto aspects, and many planets in the 8th house. These people often have a strong fascination for the past, and seem to have rewarding experience investigating past lives.

I remember particularly a client who knew nothing about astrology, but who had a strong Sun–Saturn conjunction on the cusp of the 8th house. Inspired I think by Shirley Maclaine's film *Out on a Limb*, she travelled to Europe from where she had originally emigrated to America, with the intention of delving into her previous incarnations with a psychic in Europe who held courses on this theme. She described the course as cleaning out 'past reincarnational blockages', and commented that 'for each drop shed, there was a lighter burden to carry'.

I am sure that the student of astrology here will recognise the theme of Sun–Saturn in the 8th! As her interests lay in this direction, it is of course valid for the astrologer to encourage her in her pursuit of karmic patterns from the past which affect her mood and actions in the present.

From Conception to Birth

One point of discussion amongst students or beginners in astrology is about the exact moment to be chosen for the birth horoscope. Anybody who has witnessed a birth can hardly be in doubt about this, because the moment the child first inhales air, and thereby moves from an environment of water (liquid nourishment through the umbilical cord) to the environment of air, is quite awe-inspiring. It is as if the heavens open up and life pours into the individual. The umbilical cord automatically stops pulsing at this time, so there need not be any confusion between the first breath and the cutting of the cord, as normally no more than one minute can elapse – at least with natural birth.

The question can also arise concerning unusual types of birth – premature, induced, caesarian, etc. – about whether this affects the validity of the birth chart. Research done by Gauquelin apparently seems to indicate that caesarian births do affect statistical results, although indications are weak. The manner of birth is of course very important, yet it is my contention that the horoscope will reflect all these different types of birth and their psychological consequences. Styles of delivering babies vary just as fashion does – unfortunately – and these styles are reflected by planetary trends. Births under anaesthetic are often reflected by a strong Neptune in the horoscope – and subsequent behaviour on the part of the individual which may be escapist, dreamy, unreal. Often incubator babies can be clearly identified by a strong Uranus or Pluto – especially on the Ascendant. The early days of the child are characterised by a steel and plastic artificial environment (Pluto) which has a very alienating effect later on in life. Another factor is the experience of the sudden removal of the incubator lid, with sudden dramatic exposure to background noise and voices. This unexpected change of atmosphere (Uranus) may be reflected later in a disrupted social life.

The actual birth can be a kind of mandala for the life of the child – the very scenario reflecting the coming life. My first son was born in India at sunset by candlelight, with children laughing and playing outside. Even to this day, he is a great 'candle-lighter', and functions very smoothly socially (Sun in Aquarius in the 7th). My second son was treated very roughly at birth by an unfeeling British midwife who scrubbed him heartily to remove dangerous germs. She had obviously done her training on a doll, and had not noticed there was any difference – the kind of person who says that crying is good for the lungs. Not wishing to create a scene, I held his hand throughout trying to console him. This was admirably reflected by Jupiter in Pisces in the 4th, trine the hard Venus–Saturn conjunction in the 8th.

Some people suggest that it is really the conception horoscope that is relevant, and that the birth is secondary. This is the saboteur objection – the moment of conception is impossible to measure. Several days can go by before that intrepid spermatazoon impregnates the egg. Uncertainty about the astrological relationship between conception and birth has led to a proliferation of rather simplistic rationalisations. For example that the Moon sign at conception becomes the Sun sign at birth, and variations on this theme. How can this kind of statement be tested?

Actually, it can. With recent advances concerning test-tube babies, the general period of conception has been recorded, along with the very moment of birth. Unfortunately it is apparently impossible to time the exact fertilisation of the egg by the sperm. This process is so sensitive that it has to be conducted without any light. Therefore fertilisation can only be narrowed down to a period of several hours – enough at least to give the Moon's approximate position. I was fortunate enough to get hold of this data from the hospital which conducted the first test-tube conception and birth in Denmark.

The 'conception' chart (Chart 2.1) is timed for the introduction of the sperm into the fluid containing the egg. The race is on! Of course the striking similarity here is that the IC of the 'conception' horoscope becomes the Ascendant of the birth chart (Chart 2.2). I like this symbolism, because I have always seen the IC as the source – a deep-flowing underground river which contains the roots of all things. This is the kind of correlation most appropriate to the conception/birth theme – the roots of the one forming the life-path (Ascendant) of the other. There is no correlation between the Sun and Moon.

It is interesting to note the dominant position of Chiron on the Midheaven of the conception chart – I have often noticed this planetoid dominant when high technology

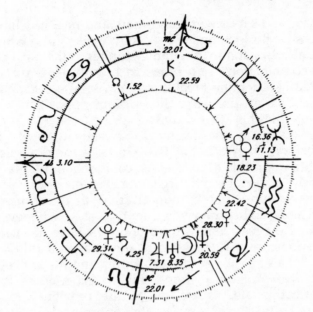

Chart 2.1: Conception 7 Feb. 1983, 17.19 GMT Copenhagen

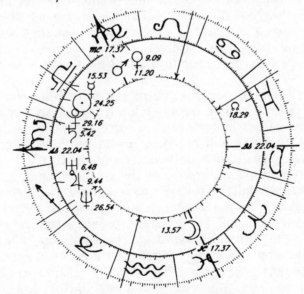

Chart 2.2: Birth 18 Oct. 1983, 8.39 GMT Copenhagen

is used, as well as with computers and health. Chiron is always worth looking at, especially when Virgo is rising. Note also the dominant Uranus–Jupiter in the birth chart. This combination often refers to heavy media influence as well as scientific breakthroughs (witness for example Prince Charles' precise Jupiter–Uranus opposition, where Uranus rules his 7th – Lady Diana).

I leave it to the reader to investigate other close associations between the two charts – for example the repetition of the Mars–Venus conjunction in precisely opposite signs, and the Virgo–Pisces emphasis.

I have subsequently noticed that there is often an interchangeability between the two axes whenever an initiated process comes to fruition, but have not yet had the opportunity to investigate the charts of other test-tube babies. Basically though, I presume the conception chart will provide a strong link to experiences in the after-death state, as well as to the previous life, and at the same time describe the enormously important events that occur while in the womb. Has the mother been drugged during pregnancy? Did she like and enjoy the child? Did she experience any sudden shocks? Did she have any strong sexual experiences? These things will have a profound effect on the psyche of the child.

Yet when the child is born, the birth horoscope will supersede any other. In principle a horoscope can be made for any major event in life. A horoscope for the start of the first school day will probably reflect progress in school, the marriage horoscope will certainly reflect the events and evolutionary purpose of the relationship. All these horoscopes will be seen to have shared characteristics, as themes from one are taken and developed by another. This concept will be apparent to all astrologers who work with mundane astrology, as a country will often have several charts, which reflect a kind of evolutionary process.

The Individual Time Journey

A horoscope will reflect the events of the present moment, and in this cross-section of space/time, the keys to both the past and the future will be revealed. This too is the principle of horary astrology, where the chart for the moment quite clearly shows the circumstances of the present, and is the key to unlocking the past and future. As children we are trained at an early age to orientate ourselves in time by studying the movement of the hands of the clock. As astrologers we have to become acquainted with another kind of clock – the vastly complicated many-handed clock of the planets, asteroids and stars.

There is a major difference between our planetary clock, and the kitchen clock. Sometimes our planetary clock-hands appear to stop, to hesitate, change their minds and move backwards. This is the extraordinary retrograde movement of the planets. In these television days, we scarcely trouble to scan the heavens and follow the movement of the planets. Yet it is a wonderful feeling to experience at first hand the movement of the planets in the night sky, to trace the formation of aspects and identify the signs of the zodiac on the background of stars. Imagine then the puzzlement caused when the observer notes that a planet which has been regularly moving in one direction suddenly reverses its movement. This is quite easy to see through simply observing the planet against the background of the fixed stars.

This phenomenon led to rather beautiful explanations of planetary movement in ancient days. Here they imagined the sphere of the planets quite correctly as separate from the sphere of stars, and performing complex loops in space.

This is a nice explanation, and from the astrological (earth-centred) point of view, quite correct. Of course we know astronomically that retrogradation is caused by the different orbiting speeds of the planets. Thus, when Venus or Mercury are between the Earth and the Sun, overtaking the Earth, they appear to move in the opposite direction, and when the Earth is between the Sun and the outer planets, overtaking them as it were, they also appear to move in the opposite direction. This means that retrograde Mercury and Venus are always either approaching or leaving a conjunction with the Sun, since they are moving, from an Earth perspective, in the opposite direction to the Sun. Similarly, the outer planets are either approaching or leaving the opposition to the Sun when they are retrograde.

It is through retrograde planets that we really confront a sense of raw fate, astrologically speaking. They refer to (a) qualities which we already have developed and have ready access to, and (b) areas in which our development is unfinished, and where we need to harvest special (karmic) experience. The first is strongly shown by the outer planets retrograde. One client I remember had a retrograde Saturn in Pisces in the 9th. At the tender age of 18 she wrote a thesis about Tibetan Buddhism (Pisces) and its traditions (Saturn) – and she herself was puzzled by her instinctive knowledge of the subject. Attentive questioning of clients about their retrograde outer planets will often reveal this 'familiarity' with the planet in question. A retrograde Jupiter in the 10th for example can show a person who instinctively gets into an expansive business venture at an early age, experiencing great success. It is as if he or she has access to talents and instincts which have existed before. Nothing new needs to be developed, it is just a question of accessing the old.

Readers are probably familiar with Martin Schulman's *Karmic Astrology: Retrogrades and Reincarnation*, and some will find inspiration from his precise interpretations of retrograde planets in sign and house. I personally hesitate to comment on the nature of past-life experiences on the basis of retrograde planets, although I have found that people have been helped by these interpretations. However, one area that is very easy to work with and check is the retrograde movement of the personal planets: Mercury, Venus and Mars. These planets provide a key to the concepts of karma and time, when they are either retrograde in the birth horoscope, or move retrograde by progression. No horoscope should be cast without investigating this progressive movement of the personal planets, as the time when they make their station, and move either retrograde or direct, is often a turning-point in the life.

Here horary astrology is very valuable for developing a sense of the significance of retrograde movement. As events in horary are mostly concerned with the immediate period of time, the course of events as indicated by the retrograde planet can be followed, and experience garnered which can later be used in an understanding of the birth chart. To illustrate this theme I would like to introduce to the reader the retrograde antics of Mercury during the year 1987. This shows the theme of crossing the time-barrier with beautiful clarity, illustrating retrograde Mercury's main job – clearing up the past.

Mercury in Deep Water

During the year of 1987 avid news-watchers were treated to one revelation after another in connection with spy affairs, undercover activity and the secret world of intelligence. The media had a marvellous time in Europe and the United States during this period. The revelations that occurred corresponded to the retrograde movement of Mercury which had occurred in water signs alone for a period of one and a half years. Mercury is regarded as 'mute' in water signs – there is no clarity of expression, feelings overwhelm intellect, thoughts dwell in the unconscious realms. Yet the function of a retrograde Mercury in water is to unearth secrets from the past, and bring them to the surface – at least whilst Pluto is in Scorpio.

A study of retrograde Mercury in current events actually provides concrete clues about hidden connections to the past and the very nature of time. In the birth horoscope the forward movement of the planets (in progressions) indicates a ripening development process. Planetary movement previous to the birth indicates prior events, and any retrograde planets at birth indicate a movement towards meeting karma from the past.

In mundane and horary astrology, aspects that have formed indicate events that have taken place, and aspects about to be formed indicate events that will happen in the future.

In February 1987 Mercury went retrograde at 14 degrees Pisces. Now Mercury is not particulary 'happy' in Pisces (it is exalted in Virgo, in fall in Pisces). Therefore this was a bad period for getting clear information – good for advertising, art and the imagination maybe, but not good for clarity. However, it was the fate of Mercury to spend over two months in this sign, so let us study its wanderings.

Mercury repeats aspects during its retrograde period three times – trine to Pluto in Scorpio, sextile Neptune in Capricorn. Furthermore it is destined to leave Pisces

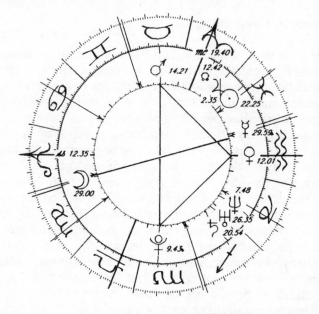

Chart 2.3: *13 Mar. 1987, 13.00 GMT Copenhagen*

and enter Aquarius, where it dwells stationary direct for two days at 29°57' Aquarius. Have no illusions that this residence in the last minutes of the last degree of Aquarius is accidental or insignificant. Sign borders are like the borders of countries – you don't just stroll over them.

I was fortunate enough to have a client at the exact time when the Moon at 29 degrees Leo opposed Mercury at 29 degrees Aquarius (see Chart 2.3). I always study the horoscope for the exact arrival time of the client, using the Astrodial (on which the planets are placed magnetically, and the movement of the Ascendant reflected by the moving dial – see page xv). This horoscope is a must for every practising astrologer – and I can only recommend the excellent book *Live Astrology* by Louise Kirsebom and Johan Hjelmborg on this subject. The Dutch astrologer, Karen Hamaker-Zondag, also writes about this subject.

Now Mercury in Aquarius indicates a surprise – retrograde, a surprise from the past, across the 2nd–8th house axis, a taboo surprise from the past (sexual, economic?). It is as if Mercury had really gone out of its way to meet the Moon, and the Moon had really hurried to catch Mercury before it left Aquarius. Leo could indicate something romantic, and Mercury in Aquarius could indicate the exotic, the foreigner, another language.

The consultation took place in Copenhagen, and my Danish client had had a sudden visit from a ghost from the past. Fourteen years ago she had fallen in love with an American in Stockholm, but this affair had been cut short at the time as she did not want to endanger her marriage. Only one day previously the man had turned up once again. Her question was: Would anything come of this reawakened love? With Venus on the Descendant having squared Pluto and moving to a square to Mars I had no doubt about the state of her marriage, and indeed she moved from home shortly afterwards after a very long marriage (an event also reflected by the transit of Pluto over her radical IC).

What particularly interested me at the time was the fourteen-year time-period, because I had seen this period reflected in many political revelations in 1987. In Britain for example the book *Spycatcher* had been published – but banned! It suggested that there had been an MI5 plot to destabilise the Labour Government fourteen years previously by bugging labour offices and left-wing organisations (Mercury in Aquarius). Later in the year an American was to write an exposé of the CIA.

The themes of secrecy, sexuality, sudden upheaval and change were constantly reiterated during this retrograde period of Mercury, basically because of the aspects made to Pluto and Neptune. In Germany in the seventies a spy scandal had succeeded in unseating the then German prime minister Willy Brandt. Information made available in March 1987 revealed that the major reason Brandt left office was because the East German spy Guillaume threatened to release compromising material about Brandt's sexual affairs. This also took place fourteen years previously – in other words corresponding to the 14 degree journey that Mercury took back from Pisces to Aquarius.

Here we are dealing with the symbolic correspondence of one degree of the zodiac correlating to a year in time. Experience shows that in dealing with the consultation horoscope and horary charts, a degree will correspond to any particular unit of time – a day, a week, a month or a year – a theme I will illustrate later.

Another secret unearthed at this time concerned the sale by a major Norwegian firm of computer technology to Russia enabling them to build new, silent (Mercury in Pisces = mute) propellers for their nuclear submarines – Mercury in Pisces (the ocean) trine Pluto in Scorpio (the ocean killer). This provoked a major crisis between the US and Norway because of American restrictions on high-tech sales to Communist countries.

But the event which overshadowed all other events at this time was the Iran/Contra scandal, and the knowledge that the US administration had on the one hand been advocating an embargo on Iran whilst, on the other hand supplying them with sophisticated weapons for the war against Iraq. These revelations led to the great media event of June/July 1987, when patriots had the opportunity to meet those national 'heroes' Oliver North and Admiral Pointdexter. By this time Mercury had entered Cancer and was racing to catch Mars (exalted in Capricorn, totally without dignity in Cancer) to bring him to justice. Mercury never did catch Mars, even though it got within half a degree. At 16°48' Cancer, Mercury went retrograde, leaving Mars to slink out into the healthier climes of Leo. It is an interesting fact that President Bush has his retrograde Venus at 17°27' Cancer, square the Moon at 17°51' Libra in the 2nd house – could there have been a secret channelling of funds here?

Having failed to catch Mars, Mercury now began a slow sentimental journey back through Cancer, where it made its station at 7 degrees Cancer in opposition to Neptune and trine Pluto. Much was revealed, much was concealed. Glamour and heroism won the day and in the end it was emotional issues that decided the Iran hearings – well, what else could Mercury do in Cancer? It took two more years before North was retried – and convicted.

In October Mercury went retrograde in Scorpio. It was destined to meet the foreboding ruler of Scorpio three times before finally leaving this sign for a year. Early in this period the weaknesses in the organisation of world finance had been dramatically revealed, as well as the extreme effect that the computerisation of the economy had on fluctuations on Wall Street.

Pluto's slow transit through Scorpio will in fact effect a total transformation of the world economy, and this will always be activated by the faster-moving planets. The market crash in October 1987 coincided with the passage of Venus (rules Taurus – therefore in detriment in Scorpio) over Pluto, and the retrograde station of Mercury at 13 degrees Scorpio. These were hard times for investors and with the major transits through Capricorn from 1988 to 1998 they will get harder.

As an avid student of the media I was most interested in what would happen when retrograde Mercury conjuncted Pluto on its way back into Libra during this period and I studied the newspapers very attentively to glean information. One event particularly fascinated me. I read that a man in America had started the engine of his plane by getting out and swinging the propeller. Unfortunately he had not put the brakes on. The plane took off all by itself and flew about 70 miles before landing relatively undamaged in some trees. The very same day a British Harrier jet, worth many millions of dollars had been observed on a rather strange course over the Atlantic. An American fighter was sent up to investigate and it turned out that there was no pilot in the cockpit. The plane eventually plunged into the Atlantic. Well Pluto does have a way of making things disappear – Pluto/Mercury is a kind of robot brain: the machine replaces the man. With the market crash in October 1987, the robot brain took over.

A most dramatic event in Europe at this time was the exposing of the undercover activities of a German conservative minister called Barschel. He had tried to discredit a political opponent through all kinds of dirty tricks until fate caught up with him. He denied that he had engaged private detectives to shadow his opponent, but in the end evidence piled up. He sought a way out through suicide, even trying to make his death appear to be a political assassination. Mercury could not pass the implacable hand of Pluto without unearthing the deepest secrets with the bitterest consequences.

Through studying events at hand, the astrologer can become familiar with the function of retrograde planets in unearthing things from the past. This is a good introduction to the more serious study of retrograde planets in the progressed horoscope, for it is through progressions that the student can truly see the workings of personal fate and karma – the harvesting of seeds planted in the past.

Beauty and the Beast

Before we consider the role of retrograde planets in the progressed horoscope, it might be valuable to look at the passage of Venus from September to December 1986. In early September she passes from the friendly climes of Libra into a nightmare landscape. In Scorpio things seem darker, feelings are no longer on the surface, demons lurk in the shadows. And what is worse – the keeper of the gates of darkness, ruler of the twilight realms of Scorpio, god of the Underworld – Pluto – is in his lair and waiting, after several centuries of wandering in other lands. This is the meeting of Beauty and the Beast: Persephone has wandered unwittingly into the Underworld.

Many months were to elapse before Venus could extricate herself from the fires and purgatory of Scorpio – months in which she was to meet Pluto three times in retrograde and direct motion – and she was permitted to depart only after she had shed every garment of false modesty, charm, sweetness and grace, emerging without her feminine wiles, but with at least an awareness of true and undying values. This was the process that millions of people underwent to a greater or lesser extent in those last months of 1986 – especially those who had personal planets from 0 to 10 degrees in fixed signs.

The main areas of trial, change and transformation were in love relationships, sexuality – and finance. Indeed in Denmark, where I practise, the government introduced a swingeing economic package at the time of the first conjunction of Venus and Pluto called 'The Potato Cure'. (This was an interesting choice of words as the potato is a Scorpio plant – riches buried under the soil.) The point of the extreme economic restrictions imposed at this time was to cut down on the enormous imbalance between spending and foreign debt. Its success was, however, somewhat limited – but this has more to do with the mischievous antics of Mercury.

In the graph (Figure 2.1) we can see the three occasions where Venus meets Pluto, and at the same time, we can note Mercury's somewhat less dignified rushing up to the very last degree of Scorpio, precipitate change of mind, quick dash back to 13 degrees Scorpio – here to make a trine to the strong Jupiter in Pisces – and headlong flight cut of Scorpio. Here I am sure we can imagine the artful Mercury quickly finding the loophole in any artificial economic package, a quick investment, and away with the profits. For my part I had visited a rather nice office in October, before Mercury went retrograde, and expressed an interest in it. Later when Mercury went direct precisely trine Jupiter, the office was offered to me. A quick look at the horary chart for the telephone offer (Chart 2.4) was quite enough for me – I accepted.

This is a classic chart. I was in a rather shaky economic position at the time – eloquently shown by Venus as ruler of the Ascendant (myself), retrograde, in fall, exhausted after two meetings with Pluto, and weak in the 6th house.

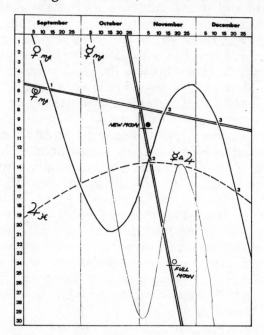

Figure 2.1: Retrograde Venus and Mercury in Scorpio, Sept.–Dec. 1986

Yet the Moon, as co-ruler of the Ascendant could not have been better placed according to horary rules. It rules the 4th, is dignified in its own sign, and is about to trine the Sun (which according to Derek Appleby almost always gives 'perfection' – success with the matter concerned). The Moon transfers the energies from the previous trine to Venus – Pluto, and finally Mercury – Jupiter, to the Sun. Furthermore the horary Moon is exactly on my natal Sun.

Note how the stationary Mercury trine Jupiter dominates this chart, because Mercury falls precisely on the angle. Here stationary Mercury shows clearly the going back to collect on an investment. (An interesting fact is that the MC is on the fixed star, Wega, 15°04' Capricorn, regarded as very fortunate for business and politics. Certainly my practice prospered after the move.)

Consultations during this period naturally reflected the theme of the retrograde Venus in Scorpio. Many people were in a deep relationship crisis at the time, often

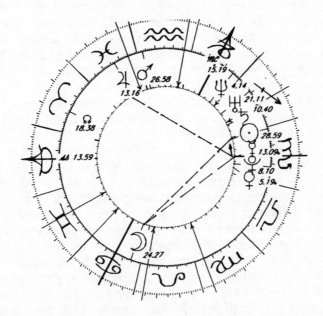

Chart 2.4: Office offer 21 Nov. 1986, 14.15 GMT Copenhagen

connected with attempts to bring new life to a worn-out relationship. Partners and lovers turned up from the past, and serious attempts were made to start anew. However, when Venus went stationary retrograde in October 1986 and then made two conjunctions with Pluto in mid-November and early December, these attempts to mend something which really was part of the past tended to abort. It was especially as Venus went stationary direct at the end of November, that it dawned on people that there was no point in wasting emotional (or economic) resources on people or things which really had to be eliminated or replaced. Thus the third conjunction between Venus and Pluto often heralded irrevocable decisions connected with relationships. Any relationship that survived this period had a good chance of a long life, but relationships based on power games, bad conscience, sentimentality, economic dependence, etc., could not continue.

In January 1987 Venus parted company with Scorpio with a new sense of realism about relationships. During this period she had also encountered troublesome squares to Mars in Aquarius (corruption, social alienation, sexual extremes in the horary chart), but had benefited from the helping hand of Jupiter – in trine from Pisces (often experienced as spiritual growth in horary charts, though rarely producing concrete benefits – trines between water signs may give emotional growth, but often involve too many dreams and illusions).

These then were some of the complex themes experienced by the consulted astrologer in the lives of ordinary people during a short three-month period. These people were responding to collective trends – transits – which activated personal issues in their own lives. These were intense months – a crisis time but relatively short-lived. But what of those people *born* in the middle of this period? What about those individuals whose very lives must unfold through progressions during those fateful days, which will be equivalent to the years of an individual's lifetime? The response of the mass to collective karma is transformed instead to the evolutionary unfoldment of the individual in response to personal karma.

Personal Fate

The older astrological traditions relied strongly on progressions as a means of prognosis, but in recent years modern astrologers have spent far more time concentrating on transits. This is because transits are more predictable. The astrologer can be relatively sure of the effect of the outer planet transits – at least from the psychological point of view – and anybody working seriously with astrology will have clients confirm the validity of transits constantly. Transits are not a perfect tool for prediction, but they are impressive. Armed with the knowledge of outer planet transits the astrologer can often convince even the confirmed sceptic by identifying periods of radical change from the past.

I personally find progressions far more difficult to deal with, and far less predictable. Transits are collective karma, which as individuals we respond to in our own personal way. Response to transits is very much based on personal consciousness, yet although the psychological effect is predictable, the actual response is less so. A person in tune with his inner rhythms and nature will sense the opportunity afforded by transits for personal growth, and use the energy to effect transitions to new states. The more resistant person can suppress the call of the planets and doggedly avoid change – perhaps. This is a very touchy point. When is it advisable to keep the ship of life on its original course, despite the transit storms in the solar system? And when should the navigator change course to tune in to new times?

The more an individual works on his consciousness and inner development, the less drastic structural change need be. As individuals we are experiencing fairly dramatic transits almost all the time, but it would not do if we were to change the structure of our lives constantly in response to these transits. It is our personal values and ethics that hold us on course, so that we do not sacrifice things of value through impulsive action.

However, I have occasionally seen strong evidence of the danger of resisting necessary change. If change is resisted through weakness – through fear of losing economic or emotional security perhaps, then the price can be heavy. I remember the case of a love triangle where the wife was so dependent on the economy and status of a husband she had never loved, that she took no action when she finally fell in love with a person who for his part left everything for her. Transit Pluto squared her Venus at this time – this aspect offers the chance to cut away relationships that no longer have any life in them – yet she dared not listen to her heart or cut away her dependence. What was extraordinary about this case was that all three parties experienced heart attacks in the same year. One can argue that it is important to preserve the integrity of a marriage – but not I think, when your life is at stake.

Dealing with progressions is more challenging. The progressed horoscope has a far more symbolic character than the transit chart, which of course reflects real conditions in the solar system at the time in question. Progressions are not 'real' in the same sense, so why do they work?

Any unit or complete revolution of time will correspond in its essential nature to any other complete unit of time. With progressions one day is said to correspond to one year – in other words one revolution of the Earth on its own axis has an essential correspondence to one orbit of the Sun by the Earth. This principle can also be applied to other complete units of time – for example one day can correspond to one lunar revolution, or one lunar revolution can correspond to one year (the two types of tertiary horoscope).

The difference between transits and progressions, then, is that progressions are unique and personal to the individual, and as such reflect his personal karma or fate. Progressions reflect the individual clock, transits the universal. To take a musical parallel, progressions show modulations in the basic tone of the birth horoscope, whilst transits show outer disturbances which either harmonise with the basic tone, or not. Transits come and go and may or may not create lasting structural changes in our lives. Progressions are a slow ripening process – often less dramatic in effect, yet more far-reaching. Aspects made in the progressed horoscope must be integrated into consciousness in a slow, karmic maturing process. Because progressions come from within, their effects are often less obvious, more subjective – whereas it is easier to be objective about the effects of transits. Therefore it is important to go into a deeper discussion with the client, to identify the developmental unfoldment of progressions.

In the progressed horoscope, rulership of the houses is the key to the effect of the progressing planets. In this sense Mars for example can represent quite different areas in two different horoscopes. Therefore a progressed Mars squaring Uranus could show the unexpected birth of a child if it rules the 5th house, or a new job if it rules the 10th – or perhaps something more surprising or unpleasant if this accords with personal karma. There are no sure interpretations of progressed aspects because they are entirely dependent on the individual chart and the complex web or rulerships. Nevertheless it is essential to combine progressions with transits in the consultation – they provide a richness of inner texture and a background of the unfoldment of personal fate.

Rendezvous with Fate

Dealing with progressions has, however, its moments of drama, especially in the case of the retrograde personal planets. Almost everyone will experience the retrograde movement of Mercury in the progressed horoscope at one time of their lives. When Mercury goes retrograde it can last for up to twenty-two years. This can mean that Mercury can wander backwards and forwards over the

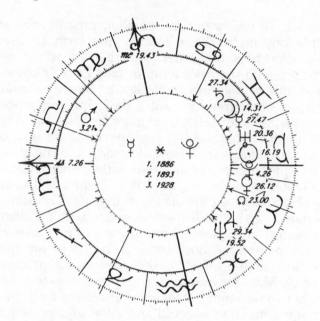

Chart 2.5: Sigmund Freud; 6 May 1856 17.17 GMT, 49 38 N, 18 9 E

same area of the horoscope for up to forty-four years. This is profoundly significant for the person involved. During the course of the life, Mercury can for example make up to three aspects with the same planet. This means that an aspect not apparent at the time of birth later comes to be the most dominant feature in the life. It is essential not to miss this when it occurs. A particular sign or house can also be heavily emphasised in this way.

Maggie Hyde in her fine article 'The Talking Cure' (*Astrological Journal* – Winter 1985) illustrates this well in connection with Sigmund Freud (See Chart 2.5). Considering his pioneering work as a psychoanalyst, one would expect some link between Mercury and Pluto, but there is none. However, Mercury progresses into the 8th house and makes its station exactly sextile to Pluto. This initiates a decade of intense discovery connected with the 'split' personality (Freud's progressed Sun conjuncts his Moon in Gemini in the 8th), and indeed the aspect repeats itself for the 3rd time towards the end of his life, bracketing a pioneering career in psychology.

In this case we can perhaps discern a purposefulness about the travels of Mercury, whose function here is to go deeper into issues, and in the 8th house to delve into and unearth the secrets of the unconscious.

There are several significant and important stages in the retrograde and direct movement of Mercury:

1. *Mercury slows in its forward motion and becomes stationary.* This is often an uncomfortable period, and there can be a sense of being mentally stifled in some way. The restless gathering of information ceases, and a more introverted state of mind is initiated.

2. *Mercury travels in retrograde movement.* Is it destined to meet other planets progressing in direct motion? Perhaps it returns to meet progressing Venus, where one would normally have expected Mercury to leave Venus far behind because of its faster motion. Such meetings have dramatic results – the hand of fate can be perceived. Marriage or love matches often occur here. What other aspects will retrograde Mercury make or repeat? Often an old theme is brought up again, an old secret brought to the surface, an old bond broken or re-established.

3. *Mercury goes stationary direct.* The karmic purpose of the retrograde motion is over, the fruits of past action have been harvested, a turning-point is reached. Ideas, research and information that have been gathered can now be distributed and shared. A mental burden is lifted, or a new start is made as a result of harvested experience.

4. *The Mercury return.* The individual can start again where he left off when Mercury first went retrograde. New territory lies ahead, totally new experiences are to be gathered. A meeting with the future. There is a sense of nervousness and unfamiliarity which causes unease or excitement. A loop of time has been completed.

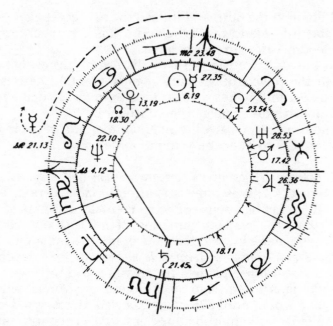

Chart 2.6: Turning-point in a politician's life

There are occasions when a personal planet makes its station in exact aspect with another planet. This is always of supreme significance. This is the rendezvous with fate, the collection of the karmic reward – or the karmic burden. On no other occasion does the hand of fate reach so powerfully into the life of an individual. When this happens, the effect is generally dramatic, and powerfully reflected in outer events in the individual's life. The experience gathered at this time may well affect the person deeply for the rest of the life. The practising astrologer must not miss this when it happens.

I have a number of examples of this happening – especially with Mercury, but also with Venus and Mars. Chart 2.6 is the horoscope of a rather infamous European politician, who was renowned in his own land for his skill in negotiating the twists and turns of income tax law. Indeed he formed a political party devoted to freeing the citizen from the tyrannies of income tax, and had a considerable following. Here we can see how crucial Mercury is as both ruler of the Virgo Ascendant and the Sun, and dominant in Taurus on the MC – a fitting position for a man whose mind was focused on the economy. Mercury is the key planet in a Grand Cross which includes Jupiter, Neptune and Saturn – clearly a man whose ideas bordered on the realms of fantasy.

During the course of his life Mercury sped through Gemini and the 10th house, Cancer and the 11th house and proceeded towards a fateful meeting with Neptune in the 12th house. At 21 degrees Leo, Mercury ground to a halt, making an exact square to Saturn on the IC, and thus activating the Saturn–Neptune square.

So what happened? (Answer on pages 49–50!).

Turning-Point

When a personal planet makes its station in the progressed horoscope, there is often an important event which has repercussions for the individual's future development. With Mars this is normally connected with self-assertion and a discovery of personal power (stationary direct), or frustration and a turning of energies within (stationary retrograde); with Venus there can be an irrevocable change in personal values, often because of a turning-point in a relationship or a 'fated' meeting; with Mercury a subtle transformation in the use of the mind – new interests can develop, new paths be embarked upon or old paths be rediscovered – a mental turning-point.

This turning-point seems to occur surprisingly often in aspect to another planet – and this other planet will describe the nature of the turning-point. I always examine even the lesser aspects – quintiles, septiles, semi-squares, etc. – to the stationary planet, because I feel that there is a purpose to this change in planetary movement; that it symbolises a repolarisation of energy and new karmic input.

Chart 2.7 is a dramatic case in point. Here Mercury has just moved retrograde prior to birth. (A Mercury that is stationary or slow in motion in the birth horoscope gives mental 'staying power', and absorbs a particularly acute energy from its degree and any aspects it receives.) At the age of 19, Mercury moved direct.

Here we can see that Mercury is placed in the 4th house and rules the 6th. It makes its station exactly on the radical Sun, therefore the nature of the turning-point is described by the Sun, and what it represents in her horoscope – creating a solid personal identity (Sun in Taurus), and communicating (3rd house). However, we can see that the Sun constellates powerfully with Pluto in the 7th (or 8th with Koch) – an exact square with an orb of only 10 minutes. Naturally we would not expect a comfortable

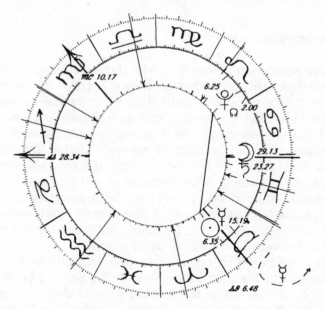

Chart 2.7: Mercury Stationary direct activates Sun–Pluto

experience here, as the Sun–Pluto square indicates deep traumas which transform personal identity.

We can imagine Mercury retrograde here as a planet with a destiny – a planet which from the very moment of birth had to collect the fruits of past actions as symbolised by the Sun–Pluto square. In this case the person in question gave birth to a mentally handicapped child – a child who obviously represented a burden to the mother, yet at the same time personified an essential characteristic of the mother's identity. The child was at one and the same time a cross to bear, and the liberation of the person involved. Her horoscope clearly indicates her fate as regards the hard domestic duties of looking after a handicapped child, and her ability to do so – the Moon on the Descendant conjunct Saturn in the sixth. Indeed she told me she found it easier to deal with these practical demands than with the more subtle emotional demands of partners.

What though was the deeper purpose of this difficult fate? One particular challenge with a mentally handicapped child is trying to communicate. The daily striving to get even the most simple message across will have made this person deeply aware of the way the human mind functions. Mental processes which we take for granted and are therefore unconscious of, will have become much clearer, and the mother will become far more aware of the nature of personal identity through the frustration of her child. Mercury's purpose here was, in part at least, to give insight into the nature of mentality. Karmic astrologers could speculate about the paying of a karmic debt, and maybe this is so, but in the shouldering of the responsibility there was also personal deliverance and growth.

Chart 2.8 shows an equally dramatic example of the stationary direct motion of Venus. Again we can see a powerful Pluto, constellating with Mars and Venus through precise trine and square. Here the 6th house comes into the picture again (illness, treatment) through the rulership of Venus. This is a sensitive and intelligent person trained as a social worker. Note the strong opposition from the 6th house to the 12th, involving Sun–Venus and Saturn–Neptune. I often find that these two houses give 'existential' crises – what is the nature of reality? Who am I? – and a strong sensitivity to other levels of consciousness, though little ability to act consciously in these areas. (More of a channel to the divine.)

Note, too, the position of Pluto in the 4th – a strong indication when stressfully aspected of trouble and alienation in family life. People with this placement need to cast away attachment to family and create their own roots – often Pluto gives them no choice. The Mars–Pluto square shows, in particular, alienation from the father. In a woman's chart this aspect often indicates early encounters with men of an extreme nature, often weak, with the consequence that they are later drawn to very powerful men, or power battles with strong men.

In this instance, however, it is Uranus that plays the

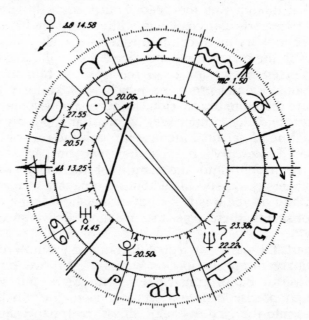

Chart 2.8: Prog. Venus Stationary direct activates Uranus

leading role, for the destiny of Venus is to move retrograde and make its station at 14°46' Aries – in precise square to Uranus at 14°45' Cancer at the age of 16! This time it is a parental crisis that creates a drastic occurrence in family life. The father is unstable and his personal crisis affects the mother so deeply that she has a breakdown and is committed to hospital. The person in question – the daughter – is so disturbed by the father's behaviour that she is sedated and committed to hospital, waking up next to her mother. The father later dies. What a difficult fate for the daughter – but certainly a fate shown quite dramatically by the heavy aspects in the birth chart.

The station of Venus square Uranus shows the inevitability of this event – the sense that a shocking experience had to be harvested as a necessity of fate. Obviously her values (Venus) about relationship and marriage will be profoundly affected by this experience, and ultimately this will affect her goals in life – Uranus rules the 10th (the parental axis). This may lead to the realisation of some untraditional ideals. On a more difficult level there can be no doubt that she has to call into question the meaning of the whole basic structure of marriage and family. To some extent this is also reflected by the Saturn–Neptune conjunction which was a feature of all births in 1953, because Neptune is not happy with the establishment of the sure structures which Saturn is normally associated with.

There is an interesting sequel to this story. Later on the daughter also married and had a child. The experience for her was so intense that she had what doctors unimaginatively call a birth psychosis. She too was committed to hospital, and the child lay beside her: an echo from the past. The 'problem' was that she felt that she had given birth to a Christ-child. Probably she was more aware than most of us, because every birth is an immaculate conception and a miraculous repetition of the Christ myth, but this magic tends to disappear in the antiseptic environment of the birth clinic and medical care. Really it was pressure from husband and family that had her committed to hospital; she was serenely communing with the gods and demons of the 12th house.

It is true, however, that Mars in the 12th square Pluto does carry the risk of obsession – and even possession by 'spirits'. The force of the unconscious is awe-inspiring with this placement. Anyone who has it would be ill-advised to take drugs in any form or to become involved in mediumship. Obsession in the case of the person discussed above could well spring from the repressed aggressions connected with the childhood trauma (Mars square Pluto in the 4th).

Generally speaking retrograde Venus in the natal chart is more prepared to experiment with relationships and get involved in untraditional forms. The individual can rarely accept the norm as far as relationships are concerned, but tends to go against convention, just as Venus goes against the normal motion of the planets. Remembering that a retrograde Venus is very close indeed to the Earth, filtering the rays of the Sun as it were, it is more pressing for the person with a retrograde Venus to define their identity through their relationships.

Chart 2.9 is an extreme example of this, because the whole theme of the horoscope is relationship. The Sun rules the 7th, and conjuncts Pluto, showing an unremitting need to define the self through breaking taboos in relationships. There are six planets in the 7th house, and the Moon is in Libra. This woman abandoned seven years of medical study only months before her final exam, left her husband and began a lesbian relationship. At this point the progressed Sun had conjoined radical Mercury only to meet progressed Venus which had moved retrograde at the age of 4. At the age of 27, this person's Venus made its decisive rendezvous with the Sun in the 7th house, leading to a major restructuring of personal and relationship values – indeed a restructuring of the whole identity. The retrograde Venus here could indicate the going against the grain by choosing a taboo relationship.

But note here that this happened precisely on the South Node of the Moon. The Nodes often show the inversion of

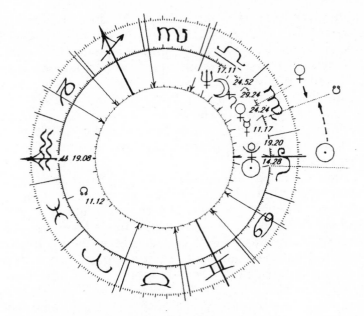

Chart 2.9: Prog. Venus moves retrograde

a principle (here the principle of heterosexuality). Indian tradition calls the Nodes Rahu and Ketu – the abortive planets. The progressed Sun on the Node is a kind of 'karmic identity eclipse'. The total identity change at age 27 was quite predictable through progressions here.

I have very many examples of the dramatic and fateful movement of retrograde Venus in the progressed chart, but we must go on to other areas. I can only ask the reader to investigate these things closely. A study of the gradual unfoldment of the life through progressions gives intimate insight into the personal karma and fate of the client. With progressions we tune in to individual time and the inexorable crystallisation of personal fate.

But what of our European politician, and his meeting with fate in the latter stages of his political career? When Mercury activated the Neptune–Saturn square he went to gaol of course, bitterly cursing his fate, and giving a very convincing martyr performance. The issue was quite clear here as Saturn on the IC does indicate the stone walls of a prison cell, and Neptune in the 12th the isolation from society – and its therapeutic effect. I remember the scene quite clearly from television – his party had pressurised him not to make any statements about his arrest and his last words (for about eighteen months at least) were 'They have muzzled me!' – a fitting description of a Mercury that has ground to a halt in the 12th, and of the sense of frustration about communication that occurs.

I have noticed other instances of imprisonment when Saturn–Neptune is activated by progression. On one occasion my client asked me how things would go for him, and deceived by some wonderful transits I forecast great success, commenting that the progressed Sun activating Saturn–Neptune would give him the opportunity to 'develop spiritual discipline'. Several months later I received a letter from him from a Swedish gaol where he was going to spend the next three years. His wife's story comes later in the book (see page 130). This proves that you should not always trust your astrologer – especially when he cannot even discover the elementary fact that you are a drug smuggler!

The Fourth-Dimensional Chart

The progressed chart shows then the ripening and unfoldment of personal karma, the ticking of the inner clock. We live our lives subjectively and intensely, and can rarely get any perspective over the hectic years from birth to death. Yet the lifespan for us is a complete unit of time, a complete cycle of development; the closing of a circle. At death we pierce the linear illusion of time, seeing our struggles and mighty battle to create identity as no more than a gossamer structure whose purpose was the refinement of the soul.

An important technique for viewing the unfoldment of personal fate from birth to death is the fourth-dimensional

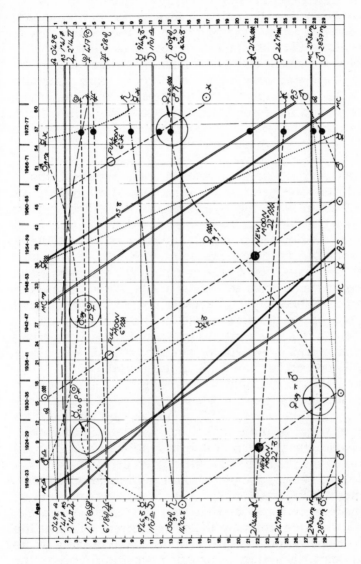

Fig. 2.2: Lifetime progressions: male, born Saturday 5 January 1918

chart, which is a graphic technique depicting the movement of the planets over, say a seventy-day period, which
will correspond in the progressed horoscope to seventy
years of the life. Astrological computer programs are being
developed which enable this graphic technique to be
printed out and will hopefully become more generally
available. Using graphs really helps identify important
years and turning-points at a glance. These graphs can
also simplify correction – major events will always occur
when the lines representing the MC/IC and AS/DS cross
planetary lines.

The graph in Figure 2.2 is an example of this technique
and in this case hand-drawn. The vertical column shows
the 30 degrees of the twelve signs of the zodiac, and
the planets are placed on this axis according to their
degree number. The horizontal lines show the unmoving
positions of the radical planets, and the diverging lines
show the progressed movement. The horizontal axis
shows the age, from year 0 to death. When lines cross
each other there is a 30 degree aspect in the progressed
horoscope – it can be a conjunction, trine, sextile, square,
opposition or semi-sextile. The type of aspect is discerned
by noting which sign the planet occupies (shown on the
right-hand and left-hand side of the graph).

Note in this example how Venus at 24°19′ Aquarius
starts off direct, moves retrograde at the age 15 and turns
direct again at the age of 56. These years were epoch-
making social turning-points for the person in question.
Obviously the final long opposition to Saturn at the end
period of the life reflects isolation and alienation here.

Note Mercury's progressed and retrograde movement.
During the years from 7 to 9, Mercury moves direct
opposite Pluto, and as this happened on the 2nd–8th
house axis, the untimely death of a parent changed the
path of the native for ever at this time. Note how Mars
simultaneously changes sign (leaving the graph at the
bottom and entering in Libra at the top). In middle age
Mars moves stationary retrograde, corresponding with
dramatic and violent events in the years of the Second

World War. Mars is later to return to its exact starting-point at the time of death.

These graceful curves eloquently describe the twists and turns in the lifetime of an individual. The fourth-dimensional graphic chart is particularly useful for mapping retrograde motion, and the example given is unusual because every planet except Uranus is retrograde or changes motion during the course of the life. Mars in particular can have a dramatic effect over a long period of time when it changes motion. Its energy is focused on the same area for a long period of time and an important karmic lesson is learned. This is normally connected with self-assertion. Particularly when Mars moves retrograde there can be Pluto undertones – the need to go against the grain and explore the unknown and taboo areas. During the actual year of change in motion a specific event often occurs. For a woman this can mean the breaking free from a man's dominant role, perhaps learning a martial art, perhaps broken bones, unpredictable events, abortion, dramatic sexual experiences, etc. People will show that they can run their own lives, and there is often a challenge to survival.

The Mars retrograde is a slow process which can dominate the whole life. In 1956 for example Mars in Pisces formed the slow opposition to Jupiter in Virgo – an influence which lasts years in the progressed chart. Typical for natives born in this period was the powerful meeting with religious or cultural men and an important spiritual or artistic turning-point. In 1948 Mars went retrograde in Leo to make a conjunction with Saturn, and for women this often meant an extremely hard testing period, and the throwing off of the yoke of domination from men and other authority-figures. Before this, in 1946, Mars went retrograde and conjoined Saturn (in Cancer this time) – in this case often bringing years of difficulty and challenge in the professional or family sphere. These fated aspects from retrograde Mars to other planets often brought men into the lives of clients, with whom there was a strong and difficult karmic bond.

Not everyone will have such profound influences from retrograde planets in their life, but those who do will have access to a profound knowledge about their past, and about previous karmic circumstances which demand their attention before they can go further in the creative process of life. Those who have few or even no retrograde planets in the natal or progressed horoscope can get on with their forward-looking plans in every area of their life. But otherwise, the retrograde planet demands a renewed focus on an old area and a confrontation with old themes for which new solutions have to be found.

Fate and Free Will

When studying progressions the question of fate and free will does come to mind. The Western mind is so anxious on this point – are we not in control of our actions? Is it not I who decides? This is not the place to discuss a subject which has been debated for two millennia or more, but I think that a misunderstanding arises about the nature of the identity. We are very far from being close to our true identity, very far from being truly close to the essence of the moment. Basically we are hardly aware of what is going on around us, so the question of free will is often not relevant. The more unconscious one is, the more predictable one becomes – the more one will react blindly to planetary forces. This does not mean that a conscious person is less predictable, however, as he or she would normally *choose* to flow with the current of time, and therefore will also be predictable.

The more aware one is of the forces of the moment, the more one realises how unconsciously we act, how automatically we are drawn into the flow of time. With all our antennae on the alert we can see how the things we do and the things we say have a kind of inevitability about them. But this does not make us weak, or mere puppets of the planets. Quite the opposite in fact – people are divine; some know it, some don't. And we play out the heavenly dramas of the spheres in acts of mythological power and significance. Working with astrology is one way of coming close to this drama.

But it is useful to believe in free will. Everybody acts as if they have it, and certainly in the astrological consultation it is wise to encourage the client to develop a positive attitude and strength of will, and unwise to encourage a fated attitude which paralyses action. The astrologer is also a part of the divine plot, and he must play his role to the full.

Sometimes, however, it can be very positive to think in terms of fate – as far as the past is concerned. When it comes to the future – better to believe in free will! Many people spend a lot of mental energy feeling guilty about actions and events from the past. 'If I had done such and such, then maybe . . .'. The conditional tense should generally be forbidden in the consultation room. Clients function better when they accept and respect their past, thus liberating the energy they waste mourning past relationships and other losses.

Being bound to the wheel of fate is the state of suffering that most Eastern religions highlight as the human condition. Only unremitting energy for spiritual growth – with a sprinkling of divine grace and magic – can liberate the human spirit from the power of karma, which binds the human to the wheel.

The progressed horoscope shows the peculiar conditions of human fate, and in this sense gives a clearer picture of individual karma. There really is less choice for a person with progressions compared to transits, because it is the subtle change of inner needs which are experienced. Free will should be practised on transits – because there is less of an inner necessity for change. Such qualities as perseverance, stability and faithfulness can forestall the outer disturbances from transits, especially when the transits activate obvious weaknesses in the chart. Transits are tests – and opportunities.

Questions that arise about progressions are for example – What happens when planets (or houses) change sign?

Are the outer planets also significant in progressions? Are progressed house cusps important? Actually, everything is significant; it depends on how much time you have to concentrate on particular areas, and what interests you most.

I remember when my Sun progressed from Leo into Virgo. Lack of money at the time forced me to take a job in a medical factory. I packed small tubes into little boxes, which I placed in larger boxes, which then were put into very large boxes. At the same time I was invited to work at a therapy centre, where I learned to co-operate with a number of different alternative therapists. Both experiences were, on different levels, very Virgoan. Some years earlier, my Venus had progressed from Virgo into Libra. At this time my job changed from sewing and designing (and organising different people in this respect) to personal consultation (Libra).

Personal experience and working with clients has illustrated this point many times – planets progressing into new signs reflect changing needs, and often this leads to significant outer change in the life. Similarly the slower-moving planets are important, even though Neptune may only move 2 degrees by progression in the whole life, or Saturn maybe 10 degrees, or Jupiter maybe 15 degrees. Their effect can be subtle and spread over many years, but it is there none the less. Sometimes events actually happen when an aspect is precise to the minute – even with the slower-moving planets. The more the practising astrologer works with correction of the horoscope (to confirm the birth time from events which the client supplies prior to coming), the more experience and confirmation he will get of these influences.

Of course, the progressed outer planets can also turn retrograde or direct during the course of the life. These planets will be retrograde when they approach the opposition to the Sun (from 60 to 80 degrees each side of the opposition) – and this means that they can change in motion if the progressed Sun approaches or leaves an opposition. I have limited experience of the changing motion of the outer planets – but it is an area worth investigating. Generally though, the personal planets have a more dramatic effect. As a general rule, changes will take place according to the nature of the planet when it changes motion. Normally this particularly affects the house the planet is in. For example a Jupiter going direct in the 8th house could perhaps lead the individual to the practice of psychology after some years of personal therapy (directing the energy outwards), or perhaps the releasing of an inheritance from a legal fund.

Working with progressions brings a richer dimension into the horoscope, and a new sense of intimacy with the element of karma and fate. Recent students of astrology have been seduced by the efficacy of transits, but in doing so often lose the mystic dimension, which progressions convey. Progressions show the individual as an active participant in his fate, trimming and improving the ship as it travels from the harbour, through outer planetary storms towards the distant destination of union with the soul.

3

Correction of the Horoscope

During the birth, which was long and painful, for my mother
made no special effort to push me out and because I did
not especially want to come out, I went on a 'consciousness
holiday' out into white light (I left the body), until the moment
when I was taken out of her body. The electric light hurt my
eyes terribly, the way people touched me was so rough and
incredibly insensitive, my nose was pushed up against an
ice-cold window. This world had no white light – oh, why
had I chosen this life in this coarse place! *NYT ASPEKT* nr. 5
1989 – Jonah Ohayv

Correction of the Birth Time

There is one area where the use of progressions is essential,
and that is correcting or confirming the birth time. The
necessity to work with correction can be more or less
important depending on where one is born in the world
– different countries have different practices concerning
registering the birth. In my experience England is the
worst.

Scotland is better, because they do keep records of birth
times. In Denmark they have an excellent archive where
birth times can be confirmed – at least to the nearest
quarter of an hour. The US is by far the best in my
experience – clients often have a record of their birth time
to the nearest minute. It is not unusual to see a certificate
with times like 5.29 or 23.46.

In all these cases, however, there is a good chance that the birth time is just an approximation. A doctor could write 23.46 because of a glance at the nearest clock 10 minutes after the birth. These minutes do not generally make a great difference to a psychological analysis, but they *do* if the astrologer wishes to make future prognoses, or if planets change houses or the Ascendant is on a cusp. In the northern hemisphere a few minutes to the birth time will not make much difference to the Ascendant degree when the signs of long ascension are rising (Cancer, Leo, Virgo, Libra and Scorpio rise very slowly over the Ascendant), but a few minutes' inaccuracy in the birth time will make a great deal of difference to the Ascendant degree when the signs of short ascension are rising (Capricorn, Aquarius, Pisces, Aries, Taurus). Indeed 10 minutes inaccuracy means a change in the Ascendant of 8 degrees for someone born with an Aries Ascendant in Scandinavia, northern Scotland or Canada.

Obviously such an inaccuracy can make a great difference to an analysis and might well mean that there is a different Ascendant. Therefore the birth time must be checked, and it can be checked. How?

The basic assertion of astrology is that human behaviour corresponds to planetary influences. Therefore changes in human life can be correlated with planetary effects from both transits and progressions. By asking the client to select four or more important events in his life, and checking them with progressed influences, the birth time can be confirmed to the nearest two minutes in almost every instance. This process of correction takes time. In the beginning it can easily take many hours to work with this information. As a bonus, however, correction work develops a strong familiarity with the influence of progressed planets in the process of correlation.

I would like to say something here about my method, but I accept that there are other methods and techniques that will also work. I use the traditional method of progressing the MC generally recommended in textbooks. This is the Naibod system, which consists simply of referring to the sidereal time in the ephemeris corresponding to the progressed date, and calculating a new horoscope with the same co-ordinates and birth time as the natal chart. Thus, to make a progressed horoscope for age 20 for someone born on, say, 4 August, a horoscope would be calculated for 24 August, same time, same place. There are other 'keys' to the movement of the MC axis (Kepler, Kundig, degree for a year) – and these keys produce small variations which become very noticeable (i.e. perhaps two to three degrees on the progressed MC) after a period of thirty to forty years. These variations can be the subject of much discussion amongst astrologers!

Correction takes so much time that it is almost impossible for practicing astrologers to find the resources to check all systems for efficacy, so they tend to stick to their own. This is fine. Life is very flexible, doing its best to adapt itself to the whims of the practising astrologer who sticks to one system. But remember: correction is a minefield where the subjective hopes and biases of the astrologer affect reason alarmingly. There is only one birth time, but experience shows that astrologers often come up with contradictory times for the same person. Therefore we must tread carefully.

Confirmation of the birth time can be obtained by correlating the movement of transits over the main angles (approximate correction), or the main angles by progression in aspect to the planets. Personal planets progressing to the conjunction of the main angles can also be used. These last two are precise correction factors. (Transits of planets over house cusps or house cusps progressing over planets can only be used as supplementary proof *after* the Ascendant has been corrected.)

Transits are useful for correction, but can only be used for approximately ascertaining the Ascendant or MC within about 4 degrees. It can be essential to do this, especially if the birth is inaccurate from half an hour to an hour each way. In these cases checking of the movement of the progressed angles gets rather difficult, because too many possibilities arise. With inaccuracies of over two hours each way even transits cannot help, because there is too much room for alternatives. There are still possibilities for correction if one has the time and patience. If it is known whether the birth is morning, afternoon or evening, then the considerable physical contrast between adjacent Ascendants can be helpful – there can be a strong contrast between baby-face Libra and dark, magnetic Scorpio with its piercing eyes; or round-eyed Pisces and sharp-featured Aries. If only the date of birth is known then I strongly recommend the budding astrologer not to waste time finding the birth time: hours can be spent, and the result will probably be wrong. By using the consultation chart (moment of arrival) it is possible to go into great detail and also to make effective predictions.

The most effective transits over the angles are those of Pluto and Uranus. Neptune will also have a dramatic effect, but things tend to be so diffuse and confused during these periods, that people may not recall the events clearly. Pluto transits over the angles have a deep effect, but people may repress the events or prefer to keep them secret. Therefore it is perhaps unwise to ask the first-time client about events connected with Pluto transits when first contacted. They may simply consider it too private. Uranus transits to the angles are almost always dramatic and liberating, and tend to be a very accurate pointer to the degree, whereas Pluto and Neptune transit effects can stretch over a couple of years and several degrees.

Transiting Saturn, Jupiter and Mars are not good enough as clear indicators of the position of the main angles, although when the Ascendant has been confirmed they can be used as further confirmation. The personal planets cannot be used, but again, when the Ascendant is known, these transits can be correlated to minor events of interest.

We will later take a look at possible effects of transits over the Ascendant–Descendant and MC–IC axes. Generally speaking, when a client rings I have keyed the birth data into the computer while they are giving me the information. A quick glance at these axes leads me to ask a couple of questions to confirm that the birth time is approximately correct. An Ascendant of 16 degrees Virgo, for example, will immediately bring to mind 1966, when Uranus conjuncted Pluto at 16 degrees Virgo. It is impossible for a major event *not* to have happened for the person at this time. If the MC is 24 degrees Sagittarius, then it would be pertinent to ask the future client whether there was a change in the career or working environment in 1987, because Uranus transited this point at this time.

Normally confirmation is forthcoming, and this has two important functions. Firstly it can be ascertained whether to make a small adjustment to the birth time when correcting the chart, and secondly the potential client feels reassured and surprised that one can see past events, and is put in a good frame of mind for the consultation.

Before going into detail concerning rough correction through outer planet transits, we can look at an example of classical correction methods using progressions. Royal horoscopes always make good examples, because the data is generally not controversial – there is a fine aristocratic tradition for making an exact record of the birth time.

Correction with Progressions

When dealing with famous people, horoscopes determined by correction are unreliable – the different techniques and whims of various astrologers result in a proliferation of hypothetical birth times. Therefore the source of information is of the utmost importance – and generally the mother, or hospital authorities are seen as the most trustworthy sources. However, even the most trustworthy sources are likely to be inaccurate. Therefore it is up to the individual astrologer to work on the data available. But recorders of birth data must stick to original sources. Bearing this in mind, I would like to illustrate classical correction techniques using Princess Diana's chart.

The data I have in this connection is 1 July 1961, 19.45

BST, 52°50'N/0°30'E. This gives a chart with an Ascendant of 18°24' Sagittarius and an MC of 23°03' Libra. This data comes from Penny Thornton's book *Synastry*, and she received the data from Buckingham Palace. We can illustrate correction techniques by choosing one event of great importance – her marriage to Prince Charles. This took place in London at 11.00 a.m. on 29 July 1981. For correction purposes the exact time, day and place is not necessary; just the month and year. If you also use tertiary progressions the date is also important. Of course one event is not normally enough for correction. This example just happens to be supported by an extraordinary number of progressions.

Progressing the horoscope by a day for a year to July 1981 gives a new MC of 13°34' Scorpio and an Ascendant of 6 degrees Capricorn. For a birth time to be confirmed the following conditions must be fulfilled:

1. The progressed MC–IC or Ascendant–Descendant must make an aspect to a natal planet. The most powerful aspect is the conjunction (opposition). Major change must occur at this time. Other important aspects are the square, the trine (sextile), the semi-square and sesquiquadrate (45 and 135 degrees), and the semi-sextile (inconjunct). There are other possibilities which might explain correlation failure when other events fit. This can be activation of important midpoint systems or the 5th and 7th harmonics – but not normally with major events.

In this case the Ascendant trines Pluto, and the MC activates the Mars–Saturn midpoint. This is *not* enough. Neither does this satisfy point No. 2:

2. The planetary pattern that is activated must reflect the event. The progressed axes precipitate events that lie latent in natal planetary patterns.

What is it in Princess Diana's chart which indicates an unusual and romantic marriage to a famous man? This is basically the Sun in the 7th trine Neptune in the 10th – the prince on a white horse. Note according to the data given this pattern was activated four years (= 4 degrees) previously. Nothing happened then.

3. Progressed planets may aspect the angles – strongest by conjunction/opposition.

Note the position of Venus in the 5th house here, not far from the 7th house cusp. Fast-moving progressed planets (Sun, Mars, Venus and Mercury) passing over the major axes are excellent correction factors. The Venus conjunct Ascendant or Descendant is a classic marriage pattern.

Points 1 and 3 are the only correction factors of importance in progressions. House cusp movement is a minor factor – although interesting.

Let's take 16 minutes from the given time. Chart 3.1 is calculated for 19.29 BST, giving an Ascendant of 15°14' Sagittarius and an MC of 18°46' Libra.

The progressed planets for marriage are placed around the outer circle. Note now how the following conditions are satisfied:

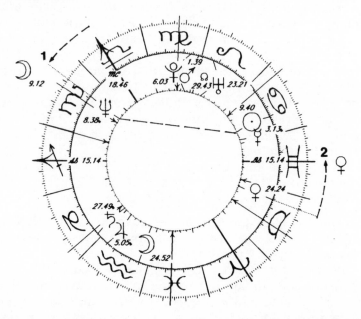

Chart 3.1:   Princess Diana: 1 July 1961, 18.29 GMT, 52N50/0E30

(a) Progressed MC: At 9°30' Scorpio this trines the 7th house Sun. The year previously it conjoined Neptune, reflecting the beginning of the relationship, escape from the press under romantic and secret circumstances (remember rendezvous in discretely parked royal train?). Note how, at the time of marriage, the progressed Moon at 9°12' Scorpio precipitates the MC trine Sun. The progressed moon is a very useful timing factor.

(b) Progressed Ascendant: At 2°06' Capricorn this trines Mars in the 8th house. Same secrecy; romantic involvement with powerful man. The aspect was exact the previous year. Notice how a year later the Descendant goes on to conjunct Mercury – the birth of a child. (At this time progressed Mercury conjoins the Sun.)

(c) Progressed Venus: Now at 15°45' Gemini – it has just conjuncted the Descendant – a strong indication of marriage.

It is rare to have such an easy correction, with so many major factors falling together at one time – but then not everybody marries a prince. Once a progression falls into place then prediction becomes a simpler matter. In this case 1981 saw the activation of a major pattern, and many years go by before another pattern of great importance is activated. This will be in 1995/6 when the powerful Moon–Uranus–Venus T-Square is activated. One would expect a change in status at this time.

For those interested in working with tertiary charts (of which there are two variations – which both work), they are often found to confirm ordinary progressions. Modern computer programs make it very easy to corroborate the correction through tertiary. Look for tertiary Ascendant–Descendant MC–IC activating either radical *or* tertiary planets by conjunction in particular. In this case tertiary MC has just conjoined Princess Diana's radical Sun (tertiary 1) and tertiary Descendant has exactly conjoined tertiary Saturn in tertiary 2. Using tertiary charts gives very precise correction.

When correcting the chart it is best to go for the simple issues which stand out. Planets in the 4th and 10th house are the easiest to deal with, because one can tell at a glance when the progressed MC–IC axis passes over them. Every degree roughly corresponds to a year. Changes in status, parental issues, work and home environment are the things to look at here. It is more difficult with the Ascendant–Descendant axis because movement is irregular, varying from 40 minutes a year to perhaps 3 degrees – but aspects here will correspond to major relationship developments. When asking for events from the client it is best to have them spread out through the life. The birth of younger sisters and brothers is always useful. Even though the client may not realise it, they probably experienced a major upheaval at this time. Furthermore they can normally remember the dates precisely. Parental moves, particularly divorce, must register in the correction. Living together with someone – and separating – will register in progressions. Apart from these events, births, deaths, travel to distant countries, illness and job change are excellent events to use for correction. Inconjuncts seem particularly common with deaths.

Armed, then, with patience and the spirit of curiosity, the astrologer is privileged to observe the unfoldment of events in a fellow human's life. When the client comes, this familiarity can be reassuring, quite apart from the fact that the events themselves give important pointers to the character and fate of the person in question. There are of course those people who have no wish to impart prior knowledge to the astrologer, and are therefore reluctant to give information. Nevertheless I will still tend to try to get dates of marriage, children, etc., from them – or other more innocuous data. With the horoscope on screen at the time of initial contact, it is normally possible to ask extremely relevant questions which evoke a willing response. Even without information, it is relatively easy to give accurate interpretation, although future prognosis can be less accurate if no correction has been undertaken. Indeed, without any data whatsoever, remarkably accurate information can be gleaned from the arrival horoscope alone – a subject which will be dealt with in more detail later.

Uranus over the Angles

The first step in approximately confirming the birth time is to look at the transits of Uranus over the angles. Generally speaking it is a good idea to concentrate on events that have happened after childhood (with the exception of deaths, parents' divorce or moving) as these are normally remembered more clearly and objectively. It is worth bearing in mind that most birth times are recorded some minutes *after* the birth, rarely before. This means that the angles are generally a couple of degrees too far advanced.

Uranus over the IC

The transits of Uranus are excellent for quick correction over the telephone so the question here could be: 'Did you move or experience any dramatic domestic changes between 1978 and 1980?' – if, for example, the approximate IC was 19 degrees Scorpio.

The actual event will have been in 1979, but it is best to ask a year either side, because the birth time may be inaccurate. The IC is very sensitive to transits of the outer planets, often signifying a complete new start to the life. It is always possible that there is no domestic change, but there is a career change (which affects the domestic life), because Uranus opposes the MC. In some cases, when questioning does not reveal any change it happens that it was the partner who experienced a career change (the 4th house is the 10th from the 7th = partner's career).

This transit will undoubtedly bring change – it is just a question of sticking to your guns and asking the right questions. In some instances the change is subtle, being more a refinement of consciousness and inner emotional roots; in other cases, the effect is dramatic – there can be short-term emigration (Pluto tending to bring irrevocable emigration), travel abroad, separation from a parent, move from one environment to another. Actually moves at this time are often connected to a restless movement back and forth. There is no stability, no rest – often great distances are involved in pendulum-like swings from one place to another.

But the final result is unmistakable. The old roots have been shaken off in a search for a more significant future. There is a new independence. It takes a year or so for the dust to settle, but new roots have been established. Sometimes there is a dramatic introduction to a new culture, or enlightening contact with foreign people. At other times there is a hectic contact with people with radical ideas about life – sometimes living in some group situation together with progressive individuals sharing similar principles.

Uranus over the Descendant

This transit is going to lead to a change in partnership emphasis. If the person is married, then action needs to be taken. The relationship cannot fruitfully develop in its old form. Unless active steps are taken for renewal, there will be explosive situations and the possibility of separation. So what should you do if it is your partner who is about to experience a Uranus transit over the 7th house? The partner will need change, and will be restless. The main thing is to encourage the partner to go out and meet new people. There is a risk involved, but there is a greater risk if one tries to continue as if no growth or expansion were possible. It would be good for example to take the initiative to go out more and meet unusual and original people, or to travel – preferably to distant, exotic lands. Old-fashioned ideas about duty and responsibility have to make way for a more flexible experimental attitude.

It may also be time to end a partnership which no longer affords the possibility for personal growth. In some cases there is no doubt that a separation is beneficial. If a person has been having doubts about the relationship for some time, this is the time when it will end, if there is no true bond.

For single people, there will also be change. On one level this can mean a new extroverted phase in the life, going out and meeting exciting people. Really this transit heralds consciousness change and new awareness through others. A single person may choose to get married at this time – but the first stage of the partnership is likely to be characterised by sudden meetings and separation. It is best under these circumstances not to try to establish a stable and conventional relationship at first, but to wait until the storm settles, and to strive to lead a reasonably independent life. There is simply too much energy and restlessness around. Probably the potential partner is unwilling at first to make a commitment. Patience yields results. Often an untraditional partnership can begin at this time – perhaps with a foreigner (and this may mean travel abroad), or even in some cases with someone of the same sex. This is the time when a person may wish to shock through his or her choice of partner.

Uranus over the MC

Generally this transit brings career change. As with all Uranus transits this can be quite unexpected. The key words are freedom, excitement and independence. Often prior to this period there is great boredom with the job.

In fact, in general, whenever anybody says 'My home/ life/career/relationship is so boring,' alarm bells start ringing for the astrologer. This is the boredom before the storm. Boredom should be translated here to mean 'I am desperate for change'. Life will oblige, and it is best to take steps and be prepared. Boredom is the barometer of change.

If someone likes their job, then this transit can mean new opportunities. It can also mean a new boss (perhaps young and innovative), who may or may not be appreciated. Often new contacts are initiated with foreign concerns. Sometimes new technology is introduced. This is the time to go on courses which give new career perspectives. There is a new need to be more socially involved.

But if a person is unsatisfied with the career, then impulsive action will be taken. The passive type may provoke being fired, the active type will not hesitate to seek new pastures. This is really the time for an individual to redefine personal goals and go for the career which particularly suits his unique talents. This can mean a period of unemployment, as traditional values about status no longer have any appeal. This is truly *the* time to actualise dreams about an 'alternative' profession.

Not all changes are predictable at this time. I remember in particular meeting a very successful person who claimed to have had a remarkable experience when Uranus transited her MC. In her birth chart Uranus was conjunct the North Node in the 8th house. When it transited her MC, a UFO landed beside her and her family in the Californian countryside.

Her family fled, but she was fascinated and actually approached the ship. Here Uranus on the MC is a literal experience – the MC symbolises what is over our heads – and Uranus, the spaceship. She actually had a wonderful, and rather famous, collection of ray guns (just toys, though! – exotic water pistols and the like) – a kind of nostalgic longing after the most significant experience in her life. The Moon's North Node shows the grounding of the energies of the solar system through the plane of planet Earth. Obviously in connection with Uranus and the 8th house there would seem to be a predisposition to experience technologies across the plane of time and space.

Actually the epoch-making conjunction of Jupiter and Uranus fell precisely on the MC of the Sagittarian-rising chart of the US in 1969, on the very day when Armstrong set foot on the Moon. (This is the 'Sibly' chart: 04/07/1776. 17.10 LMT. Philadelphia – 39N57/75W10. See Nicholas Campion, *The Book of World Horoscopes*.) The goals of the American nation at that time were to be found in the conquering of space. The consequences of this achievement for the consciousness of the world have yet to be fully assimilated – perspective over the wholeness of Earth leads to universal sharing of responsibility, and linking of the individual with the universal. The conjunction of Uranus and Jupiter at this time actually happened at 1 degree Libra – in conjunction with the Super Galactic Centre (the central galaxy around which the Milky Way is said to revolve, reflecting 'the long-term pull of our collective consciousness upwards to higher heights and deeper insights into the nature of things' – Charles Harvey, *Mundane Astrology*). At this time the Moon not only reflected solar purpose, but also higher galactic goals.

Uranus over the Ascendant

This transit signals a period of personal enlightenment and renewal. In actual fact the outer effect of this transit is not always as dramatic as Uranus transits over the other angles, perhaps because it is more personal, and less projected. However, it was for me. I remember very clearly reading one evening one of the alternative magazines from the 'Flower Power' culture in 1968, and being so exhilarated by the New Age ideas of the time, that I packed my bags that very evening, left university, and never went back. Entering the abyss of freedom.

This transit gives a chance for true renewal, and some kind of consciousness enhancement is likely – often depending on from which house in the birth horoscope Uranus comes. For example Uranus transiting the Ascendant from the 9th will probably lead to foreign travel, from the 8th, a profound psychological experience, from the 7th a new partner who turns your world upside down, etc. Uranus' effect is electric, and often comes out of the blue. Uranus puts the individual in contact with his true needs as expressed by the Ascendant. This can lead to a marked change in appearance and lifestyle.

People in stable relationships will often find the relationship come under strain, as a new need for independence and lack of interest in security threatens the normal pattern of life. Others can interpret the behaviour of a person acting under the influence of this transit as profoundly selfish. Yet the individual knows that this is the once-in-a-lifetime chance to make a radical change of direction. Someone who compromised the need for change at this time would be making a mistake – the whole future depends on actions taken at this time and therefore conventional advice from other people is not generally appreciated.

Basically all Uranus transits have a number of identifying features. They are unpredictable, they often involve contact with original or untraditional people, they bring a new awareness, they can bring long-distance travel, or oscillation between two extremes, there is a strong self-will at the time, and there is a sense of speed, excitement and exhilaration.

Neptune over the Angles

Neptune over the IC

It can take as long as forty years or more before Neptune transits over a main angle. When it does, it is a memorable event. The IC represents an individual's roots, first based in the family, but also beyond to the swollen underground river of the collective unconscious.

Here information can be accessed going back to the very beginning of human evolution. Thus Mozart, as a 4-year-old, had access to musical inspiration which transcended what was possible for a person of his years. He had a precise Moon–Pluto conjunction in the 4th, and could simply tap the resources of the collective unconscious and past incarnations. Many people with strong placement in the 4th love to delve into the past through subjects like geneaology and archaeology.

When Neptune crosses this point, the underground river rises up and overflows, sweeping away the roots of the tree of the personality as founded on parental and family expectations. Losing physical roots, the individual is forced to turn within and explore the inner emotional world. The IC is related to a need for belonging, but Neptune dissolves the old attachments that gave security and familiarity. The function of this transit is to force the individual to create spiritual roots and a new sense of belonging – to the human race and to the cosmos.

This transit will also probably affect the career in some way too, through opposition. There may be some element of insecurity or disillusion, and a need to turn away from traditional ambitions. For the person who has not allowed emotions to penetrate a busy professional life, there will be a feeling that the ground is slipping away from under the feet. Neptune wants to show firstly that there has to be a solid emotional foundation for the life and career, and secondly it likes to remind the individual that the security he spends so much time trying to establish will eventually be swept away. Life is a temporary arrangement, and it is foolish to identify too strongly with the false ramparts of our personal fortresses. From a spiritual point of view, this transit can be seen as a trial run for the death which will in the end come to us all.

Neptune does not create illusion, it reveals it. Neptune wishes only to establish clarity, but this sometimes requires magic spells and bewitchments. First a person has to be given a glimpse of the divine (reality), to awaken the spark of the spiritual search. There is one major characteristic of all Neptune transits, and that is the feeling that whatever one does to shore up the dissolving riverbanks, there can be no control over what happens. Trying to control in these instances leads to frustration, helplessness and suffering. The best attitude is acceptance – recognising something that is bigger than you, and knowing that this attitude will lead to a spiritual refinement. A meditative attitude really brings the best out of this transit.

Weird and wonderful things can happen when Neptune crosses the IC. Even under the most favourable circumstances, there is likely to be some contact with the losers in society, and perhaps drugs or alcohol. I remember vividly how this period coincided with a time of total domestic chaos for me. I rented an enormous sub-let at this time and invited an Iranian refugee (Neptune) to stay in the large flat. He had been badly tortured in Iran and sought to dull the pain with a particularly strong Danish brew called Elephant Beer. For him alcohol was a release from pain and loneliness, and ultimately circumstances fell into place for him. Obviously for me it was a sensitising time – with the rootlessness normally associated with this influence also being lived out by the people around me.

These are just some of the delights of this transit. For me it was also a professional turning-point and redefinition of my goals, later leading to work in a therapy centre, and generally getting more involved with healing.

Neptune over the Descendant

When any planet moves over the Descendant it heralds a new life-phase, when the individual, having been through a period of private integration and growth as the planet has transited the lower six houses, moves into a more outer-orientated phase making a greater impact on others and on society.

However, the first effect that this Neptune transit has is one of dissolution of existing structures in relationships. As the 7th house really represents those qualities which one tends to deny in oneself, and therefore experiences through the mediation of others, Neptune's disconcerting function is to make one aware of this projection.

The general feeling with this transit is one of lack of control over what others, specifically partners, are doing. If one has identified too strongly with the partner, perhaps moulding the partner to one's needs and expectations, or imagining qualities in the partner which he or she is not in possession of, then this transit can hit hard. I have had more than one client whose husband literally took off to sea and never returned with this transit. In one case the wife could only communicate with the husband via his mother.

On another occasion, a mother who virtually lived her life through her children experienced great suffering because one of her children (who was over 30) refused to have her interfering in his life any longer. He did not answer her letters, and refused to communicate by telephone.

These examples give some indication of the helplessness and powerlessness that can be felt in human relations at this time.

Just as Neptune's transit of the IC is a challenge to find one's spiritual roots – the inner home – the transit over the Descendant reminds one that relationships are very much projections, real enough perhaps, but transient in the greater scheme of things. To invest identity and security in another, or in a social situation, is to invite disappointment and loss at some stage of the life. The function of Neptune is to inspire the individual to tune in to his essential aloneness, and through a process of refinement awaken the person to awareness of the human plight, so that union with others can take place at a higher level, based perhaps on qualities of compassion.

It is at this time that many people come into contact with some spiritual teacher or group, who serve to heighten the consciousness. But, typical of Neptune, meetings with others can take place on many levels. Thus some may be drawn to the company of society's losers and drown their sorrows in drink, some may lose their influence by being confined (hospitals, prisons, boarding schools, etc), some may get involved with idealistic political groups.

However, any relationships formed at this time are liable to be based more on unrealistic hopes and illusions than on realities. This is the time that the young lady finds herself irresistibly attracted to the musician or artist, or where a man loses his heart to a siren. This is the time when the heart and mind open to qualities of universal love, fleetingly reflected in some aspect of human behaviour (through music, art, film, etc.), but nebulous and impossible to build on in reality. But if love brings disappointment at this time, the heart has at least glimpsed elevating possibilities, and selfless action has been evoked which in terms of the growth of the soul has great value, even if there is no concrete relationship to show for it.

Neptune over the MC

Neptune's transit over the MC will bring an element of dissatisfaction with the career. Often there is the feeling of boredom, just as with the Uranus transit of the MC, and a sense of meaninglessness about goals. 'Why am I working at this job?', could be a typical question. Now is the time to review the life goals and to try to integrate dreams and ideals into the concrete structure of life. This can for example mean that disillusion with the direction one's career is taking leads to a change of jobs – even unemployment.

As Neptune often indicates the social and professional safety net of financial support, it may be advisable at this time to choose a time of voluntary unemployment, or a job which does not pay well but satisfies inner needs. It is a good period for realising dreams and integrating a creative, spiritual or social dimension into the work. Any work connected with therapy is favoured at this time, although there may well be initial disappointment connected with realising goals. The awakening of strong ideals at this time can mean that the individual focuses on the lack of principles in the professional environment. There can be very real encounters with corruption and some of the less desirable values in the business world. This too can result in job change through disillusion.

Of course a transit of the MC also means an opposition to the IC, and indeed the whole structure or backbone of the life can change at this time. For young people there can be a change in the fortunes of one or both of the parents, and for everyone there can be an element of chaos in professional and domestic life. Neptune transits are often connected with children, mainly because the incredibly intense awareness of a baby raises the perceptions of the parents, and the helplessness of a child evokes a new kind of selfless love. For a woman this transit can signal a transformation of goals, where family values become important. I have, however, seen the opposite – in the case of a woman who gave up her medical career and left her family to join a woman's consciousness movement!

For everyone this transit gives the opportunity to take time off from the rat-race and tune into one's true goals in the context of the whole of life's journey and its ultimate destination. Not to listen to the inner voice at this time can mean experiencing a sense of meaninglessness and emptiness in the professional life.

Neptune over the Ascendant

This transit can herald one of the most chaotic periods in the life, but at the same time it is the aspect of spiritual initiation *par excellence*. It is the time when things fall apart, yet when a vision of perfection is experienced which sets the tone for the rest of the life. A powerful revision of personal values is experienced, and there is a tendency to withdraw from involvement in life rather than making a commitment to some course of action which would only cut out all the myriad of opportunities which life has to offer.

By holding back and withdrawing at this point, an individual can slowly attune to his true personal needs. Often very 'Neptunian' people can come into the life – musicians, artists, gurus, drunks – and form a part of the personal environment. Depending on which house Neptune comes from, there will be inspired activity – if it comes from the 9th, travel with a spiritual/artistic purpose, from the 10th, realignment of goals, from the 11th, involvement with musical, political or artistic groups, and so on.

A person leading a very conventional life will almost certainly experience a profound sense of meaninglessness or helplessness at this time. By undermining the secure foundations of the life role (as signified by the Ascendant), Neptune forces the individual to formulate new values and realise higher expressions of the sign ruling the Ascendant. A Sagittarius Ascendant would experience the futility of empty philosophising, and learn to integrate more subtle and flexible – and more humble – ideas into the world view. Capricorn rising would experience the unsatisfactory and illusory nature of personal honour and fame.

Neptune is not the best planet to use for correction of the main angles of the chart. It has a way of dissolving structures somewhat in advance of its arrival, and sometimes change comes some time after the transit. It is wise to give at least two years in allowing for its influence – it will certainly take that long for clarity to re-emerge. All the same it is still effective for confirming the approximate birth time, and its effect will always be felt, though perhaps not as dramatically as in the examples given. Basically it brings dissolution, and a sense of dissatisfaction or meaninglessness, coupled with a powerlessness and a sense that the hand of fate has stepped in and taken over. A meditative and patient attitude to changes at this time brings renewal and a profound sense of integration with cosmic purpose.

Pluto over the Angles

Pluto over the IC

There is probably no change more profound in life than that occasioned by this transit over the nadir of the chart. The very nature of the IC corresponds to Pluto because it refers to the roots that go back in time to a distant heritage which forms the foundation of the human race. This transit signals a kind of earthquake whose function is to eradicate unfruitful attachment to family and roots, creating the possibility for new growth. This is equivalent to the transplantation of a sapling to create new life conditions.

At this time then, the whole of life's foundations are called into question. Is the client being unduly influenced by the parents? Does early family attachment prevent the establishment of independent relationships? Can the experiences from upbringing be used in any constructive way? (Probably not at this time.) Can conventional family modes be digested at this time? (No.) What changes can be made to relieve the intense pressure in the home environment? These are some of the questions which have to be examined.

Dissatisfaction with the home-life and environment can lead to drastic change during this transit. The energy and will is there to cut away unwanted attachments. Thus I have seen a woman married for forty years leave her husband whilst in her sixties, and start a new independent life. She then lost her son quite suddenly and tragically. Yet the son had been an enormous burden on her (he had been illegitimate – Pluto – and had never adjusted socially, had not wanted to live), so in sense she was freed of all her bonds to the past, alone with herself, for better or for worse.

Chart 3.2 is of a person whose father disappeared at the age of 6 – so that he only had a very vague idea of who his father was – aptly shown by Neptune on the

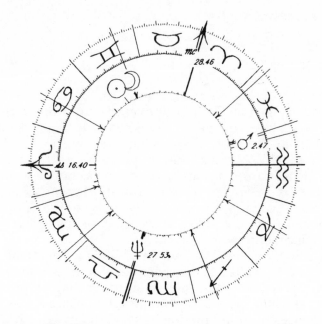

Chart 3.2: Father and son

IC. When Pluto transited this point (age 26) he chanced upon his father for the first time in 20 years. It turned out that the father was a Jehovah's Witness (Neptune!). They corresponded for some time, but eventually the son decided he did not want to continue the contact, so he broke it off.

This story illustrates an unfathomable theme with Pluto transits. They seem to dredge up unfinished stories from the past in a most mysterious way. The point of this seems to be to allow the person to re-examine and eliminate unconscious factors from the past, and finish off some karmic bond. Often with these meetings there is a feeling of emptiness or alienation after a powerful initial attraction.

Curiously at the same time this person met a married woman and had a child with her. The upheaval that this brought into three adults' lives was quite striking in that they set up a *ménage à trois*, and began a small collective farm together. It does not require much imagination to picture the stresses and strains of this family set-up, with the husband's three children and the new man and his child all under one roof! Again we can see the influence of natal Neptune in the 4th, which disposes of the man's Mars in Pisces in the 7th – chaos.

After some time the lover left the family, having sown the seed of fate for another child, whose father was also to disappear in early childhood: the family curse.

There is a general quality in the emotional and domestic atmosphere at the time of this Pluto transit. First of all there is a sense of immense emotional pressure, and a feeling that the ground is crumbling under one's feet. House owners would do well to inspect their home's foundations and take steps to make them more secure. Walls may be torn down, old rubbish cleared away. In fact there is often some unusual event connected with what goes on under one's feet. People living in a flat may experience unpleasantness with neighbours below them, or death or hard drug misuse on the floor below. There can be roadworks outside, with excavation in the street, accompanied by noise and upheaval.

Actually one of the best things one can do at this time if one lives in a house is to venture into the cellar, clear it out, and make new accommodation – this would be the physical parallel to the psychological effect of this transit: clearing away old memories and exploring the unconscious, discovering new possibilities for growth. One man I knew established a study in his cellar, where his son spent all hours of the day and night experimenting with his computer.

On occasions there can be a move and change of job at this time. Normally the move is drastic – from one environment to a totally new environment. This is the time for emigration, when the roots in the home country are totally dissolved. Young people still living at home will definitely move out, younger children may experience a death in the family or parental divorce, or a move. Married couples may decide to start anew somewhere else – with or without each other. Or the partner's job may be affected, pressure at work contributing to a difficult and intense time at home.

But the basic challenge of this transit is to learn to stand on one's own two feet, to eliminate old support structures (which have their emotional price), to delve deep into unconscious behaviour based on past conditioning, and to create a new emotional and physical foundation for one's life.

Pluto over the Descendant

Obviously this transit is going to change the basic way you relate to others. Thus those who have no nameworthy attachment at this time will experience a very intense relationship. Those who have a relationship will experience a period of up to two years in which the whole foundation of the relationship will be called into question. It is a make or break aspect. This certainly does not necessarily mean separation. I remember one example where the married coupled decided that their relationship needed some kind of renewal and took a long trip to Thailand. One day, whilst sailing off the coast, they ran into a severe storm, and their boat started sinking. They had actually said their goodbyes to each other, but were saved at the last moment. This experience really cemented their relationship.

However, a relationship which is weak cannot survive this transit. Pluto always brings the theme of power and power misuse into sharp focus, and often there are powerful sexual themes evident under this transit. Certainly the individual is inclined to go much farther than normal in investigating what is acceptable and what is taboo in a relationship. Economic themes can also be apparent, and this is the time a person will shake off economic dependence on the partner, and the subtle manipulation that goes with it.

Sometimes the partner will go through a mental crisis or breakdown, thus confronting one with the abyss of the fine division between sanity and madness. In a sense it could be said that the partner is doing one the favour of living out personally a mental torment which is also highly relevant to oneself. The question arises of course whether one's own behaviour may be a factor in this. Jealousy and control, a refusal to examine emotional issues in depth and a rejection of the magical may all be factors that contribute to mental imbalance in the partner.

This transit is very likely to bring Scorpio-type people into the life. This is the dark and passionate type, the magician, with sexual charisma and magnetic charm. There is an irresistibility about relationships begun at this time, and a sense that one has to get involved, even if reason advises against it, fascinated as a moth is around a flame. A compulsive attraction and sexual fascination drives a relationship on and on, even though there is a feeling of utter exhaustion. Humiliation and power battles become important elements in a relationship, until one takes the final steps to eliminate an emotional connection. A marriage that ends under this transit is accompanied by intense emotional scenes, separation, powerful sexual reconciliation; then peace leading to unbearable intensity, crisis – until bonds are finally cut. A relationship finished at this time is normally irretrievable, and often there can be great difficulty in forgiving the erstwhile loved-one.

Another phenomenon connected with Pluto's transit of the Descendant is the inexplicable disappearance of the partner. A relationship can end without warning or explanation – through inexplicable psychological factors or the personal fate of the partner. Pluto can very much be the implacable hand of Fate, an alien force, which confronts the individual with the experience of emptiness.

After this transit past modes of relating are changed for ever – there is no desire to waste time on trivial relationships, it is the burning issues of soul evolution that become important. Therefore meetings have a new and more profound significance, and many past social connections fade into the background. False projections and expectations connected with partners are ruthlessly eliminated, and those connections that remain are strengthened and deepened.

Pluto over the MC

The signature of this transit is career pressure with probable job change. One feature of Pluto transits is the feeling that there is some form of secret conspiracy. There can therefore be a feeling that job competitors are siding against one, or that one is up against insuperable odds in the career. This is the time when one can be confronted by professional superiors who act in a autocratic and unfeeling way. Whatever the reason there tends to be a sense of exhaustion about the job – a feeling that one cannot continue one moment longer, yet a sense that nothing else exists to replace this position which one has worked so hard for.

The reality in some cases is that a job transformation is a virtual necessity. On occasions there can often be an undercurrent of corruption or criminality which it is wise to distance oneself from. It is worth remembering that the Watergate crisis happened when Pluto transited the MC of the Sagittarian rising chart of the United States, and here we could see all the ingredients of executive power misuse, criminality, secrecy and manipulation that can characterise this transit.

The most important thing is to find a job which involves one totally – anything less will be boring and unsatisfactory. Personal commitment and all-out effort is essential. Often new careers started at this time can involve computer technology or psychology in some way. This is the very best time to make a total transformation of one's goals – especially if one has been pursuing a

6th house type of career, working to satisfy the needs of others.

It can be difficult to salvage honour and reputation at this time, or the individual can be tempted to stoop to low measures. Pluto can be connected with both the police and the underworld, and contact with these forces at this time cannot be recommended! One acquaintance of mine worked in a computer firm during this period, but, having purchased his own home computer at this time he spent days and nights totally absorbed at home instead of turning up for work. Naturally he was fired. Having a fairly strong Mars–Pluto aspect (revenge!) in his horoscope he spent many a long hour brooding over how he was going to plant an electronic 'bomb' in the computer system of the company.

By programming in this bomb before he left he could arrange for all the files and information in the firm's system to disappear when a certain date was reached – long after his departure. His partner eventually dissuaded him from this folly – yet we have here nicely illustrated the themes of the electronic world, hidden destruction and revenge which so often accompany Pluto aspects.

As with all transits of the MC–IC axis this transit brings the opportunity to transform the life-structure. This axis is the backbone of the chart, and I have sometimes quite literally seen work on the back during Pluto transits here. Especially recommended would be rolfing, chiropractic and other structuring massage. By accepting the challenge to realign the goals and structure of the inner and outer life at this time, the path is set for future success and honour. It is a very hard-working period, but often great success comes just after this transit.

Pluto over the Ascendant

Many people with Libra and Scorpio rising (and in the northern hemisphere there *are* many) will have experienced this transit throughout the seventies and eighties. The radical transformation of relationships has been clearly indicated by Pluto's transit through Libra, and it is at this time we have experienced experimentation with for example homosexual relationships – reflecting Pluto's associations with decadence and the 'taboo'. All transits of the outer planets over the main angles are modulated by the sign on that angle, and there will be very different experiences dependent on this sign.

One feature that is universal with Pluto's transit of the Ascendant is the intense pressure that arises at this time to tune in to the essential role in life. There are periods of intense activity, coupled with periods of total exhaustion – this can sometimes mean an apparently inexplicable need to sleep long hours to recharge one's batteries. As the Ascendant also represents the personal appearance, there can be radical changes in looks. Fat people may go on a radical slimming programme, bad habits can be eliminated. Sometimes the personal name is changed – nicknames are taken on or eliminated. Teenagers will turn punk, adults will take an uncompromising stance about their future life-path. With all Pluto transits the issue of survival rears its head – changes come not because of whims or fancies, but because the very life depends on it.

Many events can be associated with this transformation of identity. One friend of mine travelled to Israel at this time (during the invasion of Lebanon – guns, bombs and terrorism), and liked it so much that he considered changing his identity and adopting the Jewish faith so that he could remain in Israel.

Other people who have lived a single life for many years may choose to marry; married people may choose to be single. The choices made at this time will set the pattern for the future. This is a major period for gaining deep psychological insight and perhaps to experience personal therapy. At this time there is a sense of fate stepping in or intervening – rearranging life's structure in a more meaningful way. Superficiality is eliminated, and life becomes deadly serious. The will to change is all-encompassing and there is little room for compromise.

Obstacles can seem insuperable at this time, but at the same time the personal survival urge and strength of will is at its peak. 'Where there's a will, there's a way' is the key expression for this period of the life.

With all Pluto transits there are certain common features: There is pressure and the struggle for survival, encounter with power structures, profound sexual experiences, economic struggle, secretiveness/alienation and the elimination of past attachments, intense activity and exhaustion. At the same time there is a sense of rebirth, new life and hope, and a new strength of will and purpose.

4

Consultation Time

... the great globe itself,
Yea, all which it inherit, shall dissolve,
And, like this insubstantial pageant faded,
Leave not a rack behind: we are such stuff
As dreams are made on; and our little life
Is rounded with a sleep. *The Tempest*. IV. i – Shakespeare

Humble Beginnings

At some point the budding astrologer encounters the
hurdle of the first consultation, if he or she is the
type who is motivated by human contact. Normally
of course this is a soft transition process with many
an experiment on friend and family before the jump
is taken. But the first time money is exchanged and
professional services offered is a kind of turning-point.
It is also important for the client because human nature
is such that people appreciate things more when they pay
for them! And as every psychologist knows, a consultation
works better when it hurts the pocket. Clients don't like to
waste precious time.

Each client is also a teacher adding to the expertise
and store of knowledge of the practising astrologer. The
meeting between astrologer and client is normally fortui-
tous for them both, and comes just at the right moment
for their mutual consciousness development. It does not
take long for the busy astrologer to realise that clients

come in strings often illustrating a general theme that is interesting the astrologer at the time. The astrologer's work will seldom bring riches, but a greater reward is gained – the work keeps him finely tuned to the essence of time, tuned to the magic of the moment. And at the same time he learns of and shares in the limitless fate of humans and of the human predicament.

In the first nervous beginnings in the profession the astrologer is inclined to stage the consultation as a monologue, in which the client is fed with a long exposition of the horoscope as a collection of planets in houses and signs in a myriad of aspects to each other. The helpful client may nod the head and grunt occasionally and perhaps eventually settle into a friendly chat with the astrologer. No magic has happened. No transformation has taken place. At the very best the client has had confirmed what he already accepted – that he is a part of a greater whole, and responds to the movement of the solar system. And if the astrologer has been talking all the time he will have learned nothing new.

Some clients – especially those with strong Scorpio and Saturn influences may indulge in obstructive tactics and it can pay to confront this type of client right at the beginning of the consultation with their tendency to sabotage the very consultation they are paying for by not being open – Scorpio, for example, respects power and directness, yet is very afraid of being vulnerable.

If only conventional astrological techniques are used, problems can also arise when direct questions are posed. Should I sell my house? Should I take this job opportunity? etc. With transits and progressions at your disposal, even with tertiary horoscopes or Solar Returns it is incredibly difficult to identify specific themes relevant to the present reality of the client – and to comment on how they will develop. The astrologer can talk of trends, and loves to dwell on psychological themes (though is rarely qualified as a psychotherapist) but may be lost as far as the everyday reality of the client is concerned.

But it is this everyday reality that is of the utmost importance. Every little event in the client's life is the pure essence from the crucible of karma – a specific clue as to the nature and fate of the client, a test and a chance for consciousness and growth. The houses of the horoscope show where, when and how this event takes place – they are the finely woven web of crystallised karmic energy. Events in the life as reflected through the houses offer the magic code which breaks through the chimera of so-called reality, which ultimately is a complex projection whose roots lie in personal karma.

Without the techniques of horary astrology as used in the consultation horoscope the astrologer runs into considerable difficulty with a certain type of client – in particular the businessman. This person is not normally so interested in being psychoanalysed and may indeed take offence if he is; neither is he interested in being told about personal karma, esoteric truths or spiritual development. Why should he be? He does what he is good at, whether it is making money, administering people or resources, or whatever. He has to be communicated with on his own terms. Perhaps the astrologer is not interested in business, power or acquisitions, yet, if the *consultation horoscope* is used, there will always be a meeting point between consultant and client. After all they are both contained in the horoscope for the moment of meeting, with the 1st house symbolising the client and the 7th house the astrologer (amongst other things). Furthermore the choices and dilemmas in the business life of the client will reflect major life issues which also have a 'spiritual' angle. The consultation horoscope is the magic tool available to every practising astrologer for revealing the mysterious interweave of events. In this connection the *Astrodial* is an invaluable instrument, and will be described later.

The Magic of Meeting

The potential client has telephoned you, you have taken the birth data, and if you are a conscientious astrologer you have probably tried to corroborate the birth time by matching it with the events in the subject's life. A meeting has been agreed on and you await with a certain element of suspense the arrival of the client. After all you may have already spent several hours working on the chart so you feel as if you know the person quite well.

The person may be delayed: perhaps a child has suddenly been ill, the wrong bus has been taken, maybe there has been confusion about the address. The client may ring at the last moment and cancel, or may have turned up early. On the day the client meets astrologer all events leading up to the meeting have profound significance and can be used to shed light on interpretation. When the doorbell rings and you greet the client on the threshold a horoscope of importance is formed – the consultation horoscope. The wide world outside is the Cosmic Womb, and when the client crosses over the astrologer's threshold he is born once more.

Perhaps it would seem at first glance that this meeting time is a simple accident. You had your part in arranging it, just as much as the client. If the client was delayed by a bus strike then isn't the consultation chart invalid? Yet experience shows time and time again that the moment of arrival is no accident: the client may be early or late, but always comes at the right time. The horary chart for arrival will reflect in exquisite detail the major circumstances of the person's life, certainly at that present period, but often of the whole life. Such is the potency of the First Meeting chart. Sometimes arriving late means that the Ascendant will change, or that planets become significant through cunation on a major axis or house cusp, and these factors will change the prognosis considerably.

In a way it is a puzzle that the consultation horoscope has received so little attention. It is a big subject in itself, and a very few modern astrologers have written about it.

A few hundred years ago, however, the consultation chart was the basic chart used. Few people had a knowledge of their birth times so the astrologers of the period – and there were many – cast horary charts for the client's arrival. One of the best-known was of course William Lilly, whose book *Christian Astrology* has recently been reprinted by Regulus Press. The details that these astrologers went into were extraordinary and their accuracy was mind-boggling. And they did not use Uranus, Neptune and Pluto.

It is important to wait to make the consultation chart until the moment of arrival. It cannot really be drawn up in advance, because the arrival time is uncertain, and delays are very significant. So if you have a computer you could perhaps make a quick print-out at the moment of arrival, yet in a way it is a pity to destroy the first magic moments with something as noisy as the average printer. I use the Astrodial, which is a very aesthetically pleasing instrument on which the planets are placed magnetically, and with an inner disc which can be turned reflecting the movement of the Earth and thus the changing degrees of the Ascendant and houses. It creates an instant horoscope without fuss and noise and it is delightfully tactile. Planets can be moved backwards and forwards to demonstrate important points – it is the perfect interface between astrologer and cosmos. This is the tool that cuts through the iron reserve of Capricorn, and the fanatical secrecy of Scorpio! This is the tool that makes you gleefully await the high-powered businessman client whose time is money! The birth chart may reveal no transits and progressions of importance, but the Astrodial will reveal all; it is the passport to travel in the client's world.

The Client Appears

The doorbell rings then, the client enters, and the consultation begins. These first moments can be savoured. What is the client wearing? Colour choice can be incredibly revealing, and is generally more varied if the client is female. A person dressed totally in black is often in trouble, for example. This might be because black absorbs light, and this person is feeling at a stage of life when she feels she has little energy to give.

Choices of blue and green show the person who feels more integrated, or striving to be integrated and accepted, medium greens in particular showing a soul in balance. Warm pinks will definitely show the romantic and inviting type, whilst whites and lilacs will often indicate a person who goes around idealising things without adequate personal grounding. Stripes and spots will also tell their story – horizontal stripes in particular indicating a person who tends to get into confrontations. Stripes are indications of a Uranian influence, with diagonal stripes tending to shows a less confrontational person who still wishes to signal that he or she has a unique viewpoint. This will be especially marked when asymmetrical styles are chosen. Obvious display of labels (which has been especially marked since Neptune came into Capricorn) or sharply tailored clothes may well show a Saturnian influence; bold emblems will indicate a strong sense of self-importance perhaps reflected by a strongly aspected Sun. There are of course countless variations and I name here but a few. It is simply good training for the astrologer to learn to correlate personal appearance and style with the horoscope.

Jewellery is also extraordinarily revealing, reflecting both personal values and taste, and attitudes to magic and power. Rings are a study in themselves – from the more extreme situation with a ring on the thumb (power use and misuse, abdication of personal will to a higher force) and the index finger (very strong opinions or ideology), to the more normal choices of a ring on the third finger or, more unusual, the little finger. The tradition for placing a ring on the third finger of the left hand when getting engaged or married shows this finger's obvious correlation with love and relationships. Choices of coloured stones often speak for themselves here. I have seen for example large black stones on this finger in connection with denial of love or tragic events in connection with relationships. One client had a black and white stone in a ring on this finger and this related quite clearly to the dominating Venus–Pluto opposition in her chart which fell on her 5th–11th house axis. After this client had separated from her husband, one of her two children had 'chosen' to live with the father. This separation had taken place over a matter of 'principle' – but the astrologer can sense here the emotional ultimatum (Venus–Pluto) that the mother herself had given, with the self-destructive consequences often seen with Pluto. A strong Pluto often indicates the subject seeing issues as black or white, and this can be reflected in personal taste.

Earrings and pendants will also tell their story, as well as choices of motifs for brooches, etc. Occasionally a person will come who is overladen with jewellery. I notice this particularly when female clients have Venus–Pluto or Moon–Pluto configurations in their charts, or, more collectively, when Venus makes its yearly transit through Scorpio and therefore affects the consultation horoscope. Often this type of person will use a heavy perfume also, which I assume is a reflection of the anxiety about feminine self-worth and sexuality that this influence can cause. Heavy jewellery also brings issues of power, magic and sexuality to the fore.

Of course these personality traits should also be visible in the birth horoscope, yet it would be foolish to ignore the obvious signals the client deliberately sends out. Strengthening personal observation enriches daily life experience and expands astrological intuition in situations when the personal horoscope is not available.

The Astrologer as Magician

The average client believes in astrology and does not need much convincing. Some, however, are extremely sceptical – and why not? There is no reason to believe in astrology if you can't see it work. Even those who do accept it rarely grasp the entirety of the field of influence planets have on their lives. Men in particular are afraid to seem foolish and often deride astrology because of peer pressure. Especially people with an analytical or scientific frame of mind are ill-disposed towards astrology. After all much of their world system is threatened by it. Sometimes even their job can be at risk if they openly are seen to accept astrology. I can remember having as client the assistant editor of a scientific magazine who was very concerned that any of his colleagues should discover that he had had his horoscope done. The central focus in the consultation was one of co-operation with a fellow editor. Ironically enough the fellow editor was a regular client of an astrologer friend of mine who was equally concerned should her interest in astrology be discovered at her place of work!

It is important that this type of person has a convincing first meeting with the astrologer and the horoscope. Therefore it is essential to make an impact at the beginning. To list the qualities of clients in textbook form only serves to build up a wall of politeness or defence. When the client enters and takes a seat he or she enters a magic world where time is suspended. True, spiritual issues and psychological insight are important, but then the person could have booked time with a clairvoyant or a psychologist. As an astrologer it is your job to blow away the cobwebs from the mind in true Uranus style. You should be able to come up with the unexpected; you should be able to give a surprise!

What better surprise then than to tell the client what is on their mind at that very moment in time, relating the issues that have led up to this and giving a broad view of how they will develop. Later you can go into psychological depth as to *why* the client encounters this kind of problem or incident at all, but in this first magic moment perhaps you should show your client your credentials as an astrologer.

This is the astrologer as magician who cuts through suspicions and defences at the start so that precious time is not wasted during the remaining one to two hours.

Accuracy at the beginning encourages the client to be open, and being open is a prerequisite for discovery and growth. This is especially important when dealing with people who have strong Scorpio, 12th and 8th house and Pluto influences, and those with strong Saturn influences. If these people at the beginning feel that the astrologer has an intimate knowledge of their inner life, then they will open up and have a rewarding experience; if they do not, they will not reveal anything. By putting your cards on the table, revealing the power of the consultation chart, a strongly energised atmosphere is generated.

Using the Astrodial and consultation horoscope it is surprisingly easy to specify details of the current situation in the client's life. Not only that, details about the partner, children and parents and their lives can often be accurately related by simply turning the horoscope around so that the relevant house shows on the Ascendant (i.e. through derived houses). Problems in your home environment will be magically reflected by challenges in your partner's career (4th house = partner's 10th). Plans to travel abroad may mysteriously correlate with changes in a sister's partnership situation (9th house = sister's 7th). This system can be seen to work and has important philosophical implications as far as life-experience is concerned.

Interpreting the Consultation Chart

Generally speaking the rules concerning interpretation of the consultation chart are similar – but not identical – to those of horary astrology, with a few modifications, and there is plenty of good literature on this subject. One can view the arrival of the client as a big horary question. I do not wish to go through all the details of horary here, but simply wish to mention some basic points and some observations based on experience.

The Ascendant represents the client and will basically show the tone, style and appearance of the client, manifesting strongly in the way the client communicates and in the subjects the client concerns himself with: there will be a natural charm and nobility about the client when Leo rises, and perhaps the concern will be love, romance, creativity or children. Scorpio will show a more controlled and secretive nature with focus on taboo issues, security, sexuality, etc. There will almost always be a secret to get to the bottom of here.

Of course the Ascendant influence will be powerfully modified by the position of the Ascendant ruler – and here it is important to remember the rules of horary as regards using the traditional sign ruler – Mars for Scorpio particularly, but also Jupiter for Pisces, and Saturn for Aquarius. The sign position of the Ascendant ruler will give additional detail about the character and personality of the client, and the house position will without doubt show one major area of interest which will be deeply discussed during the consultation. This is the most personal point in the consultation horoscope.

The Sun is more of a general factor in the consultation chart, often representing figures of authority and respect. Here it is wise, however, to remember the rules of exaltation, debilitation and fall, for experience shows that even the Sun can lack dignity and honour when in Aquarius (debilitation) and Libra (fall – where it can often signify the immature romantic, or the person who compromises honour for acceptance).

It is the Moon which is of profound significance, always showing the major area of absorption and focus. Through the Moon, planetary energies are distributed throughout the chart – it is the chief significator of the unfoldment of time, aspects that have been formed indicating events that have taken place, and aspects that are to be formed, before the Moon leaves the sign it is in, showing events that will take place in the future. The Moon shows quite clearly the emotional frame of mind the client is in, and the current area of attention.

Mercury shows the state of mind of the client, and here the horary rules about a combust planet (i.e within $8\frac{1}{2}$ degrees of the Sun) apply. The closer Mercury is to the

Sun the greater the worry and intensity of mental focus, growing as Mercury approaches the Sun, and easing up as the aspect wanes. There is a horary expression, *cazimi*, when a planet is within 17 minutes of arc of conjunction. Here a planet is said to gain strength, and my experience corroborates this, at least with Mercury. The mind of the individual is in the eye of the storm and great insight into the nature of life and identity is often demonstrated by the client, although it is a brief respite in a broader situation of mental turmoil.

Venus has much to do with material things, but often also represents on a broader level the kind of woman talked about during the consultation – whether it is the client herself, or other women that come into the story. The same applies to Mars and men and indeed the polarity of Venus and Mars in the consultation horoscope is a fascinating study, dealt with at the end of this section. Venus in Pisces will tell the story of the dreamy and idealistic woman who sacrifices herself for the principle of love, whilst Mars in Sagittarius would for example symbolise the man who travels the world in restless quest, refusing to be tied down. For the practising astrologer, watching the wanderings of Venus and Mars through the signs reflected in the love-lives of clients and their partners is a fascinating experience.

Every day for weeks at a time variations on the same theme are described by clients so that the astrologer gains a deep experience of the meaning and influence of the planets. There is no better teacher than the consultation chart, brought to life by the story of the client.

Sign Boundaries

As mentioned before in the section on retrograde planets, experience shows that the border from one sign to the next is razor sharp; in horary astrology at least one cannot talk about the gentle transition of a planet on the cusp. Normally in horary the focus is on the Moon, the rule being that when it leaves a sign there will be no further development of the issue under discussion. If the Moon makes no further aspects before leaving a sign, it is said to be 'void of course', although William Lilly's experience was that this might not be the case when the Moon was in Taurus, Cancer, Sagittarius or Pisces – in other words it is wise to be flexible about this rule.

With a void of course Moon the horary judgement is that there will be no further developments in the matter, either positive or negative. In the consultation chart one can add the proviso that if a person wishes to achieve something when the Moon is void of course, then he must wait until radically new circumstances develop, reflected by the new sign the Moon comes into. When the Moon is about to change sign around the time of a client's arrival there can be no doubts that new circumstances and needs will arise. A person who comes with the Moon at 27 degrees Gemini for example will soon be feeling the need to reject an intellectual and dispassionate approach in favour of emotional needs (Cancer). The person may, for example, wish to settle down and start a family, or to leave studies and work at home.

The Moon is the major instrument of timing in horary and a degree will often represent a month (but can also represent a day, a week or a year – or maybe all of them, such is the mysterious nature of time). The degree orb of aspects made by the Moon will often reveal the number of months ago an event occurred in the past, whilst degree orbs for future aspects will reveal the number of months that will elapse before a future event occurs. Future aspects taking place *after* the Moon changes sign will still symbolise future events, but timing factors become more confused. The Moon moving from Aries to Taurus would be changing to a lower gear as it were. Timing is complicated in horary, many factors have to be taken into consideration. I certainly have not mastered this yet.

Other planets changing sign also show deeply significant transitions. The observant astrologer can draw

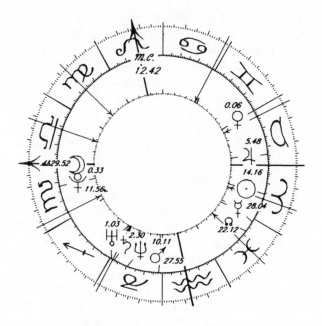

Chart 4.1: 3 April 1988, 20.30 Alrø, Denmark

inspiration from everything around him to gain experience here – including television. It would appear that
the people who organise programmes many months in
advance of the night must be master astrologers. How
else can one explain the fantastic correlation between TV
programmes and astrological configurations? Watching
Educating Rita one night on TV (starring Michael Caine as
a drunken university professor), in which a working-class
girl abandons her job in a beauty parlour to take a degree at
university I was struck by the fact that Venus had changed
from Taurus to Gemini in the very minutes prior to the
start of the programme.

   The chart for this moment (Chart 4.1) is a study of
sign change, with the change of Ascendant from Libra
to Scorpio showing Rita's exit from her safe working-
class marriage. The theme of personal transformation
is clearly shown by the Moon rising in Scorpio on its

journey through the Underworld it dreads (in 'fall'), to meet the lurking monster Pluto. Rita's husband is enraged by her clear dereliction of duty as mother and housewife (she hides her secret supplies of the Pill under a floorboard, having no intention of becoming pregnant – good Moon–Pluto stuff here) – and during his rare appearances in the film is seen tearing down walls and floors whilst rebuilding their house.

The strong 3rd house shows her hunger for knowledge, and the revolutionary effect it has on the structure of her life (Uranus–Saturn). She meets her drunken and disillusioned university professor (under the Open University scheme whereby ordinary individuals can embark on university degree courses) – symbolised by Mercury in Pisces perilously close to the unhappy star Scheat (29 degrees Pisces), and disposed of by Neptune in the 3rd house. As we can see, Mercury and Mars are both about to change sign, so there is hope for our drunken professor. At the end of the film he leaves his boring university job and starts a new – and sober – life in faraway Australia (Mars goes from Capricorn to Aquarius, and Mercury from Pisces to Aries: the liberated pioneer).

This transition of Venus from the material and sensual Taurus (from the beauty parlour to the university) reflected for me a dramatic shift in female client type over the next three months, when Venus went through to the end of Gemini where she flirted with the idea of family bliss (went stationary retrograde at 1 degree Cancer opposite Uranus 1 degree Capricorn), and shocked by her traumatic meeting with Uranus returned to the cooler intellectual climes of Gemini, resolutely refusing relationship commitment. April to July 1988 was the summer of the single girl determined to improve her mind (see page 154).

Sign change shows then a radical shift of focus – it is really marked in the consultation chart. A planet at the end of a sign is satiated, and this can reflect a feeling of boredom or pointlessness in the client's life (if the planet is Ascendant ruler – otherwise it will reflect circumstances of the house it is significator for): what more is there to do?

A planet at the beginning of a sign is fresh, but naïve and immature: what is in store for it?

Exact calculation of the Ascendant and MC is important because when the client comes at a time of shift in the main angles of the consultation chart, there will be major new circumstances arising. Generally one degree will indicate a month here – these axes are major timing factors. Therefore if a client is toying with the idea of changing job or moving, and the MC–IC axis is 29 degrees of a sign, you can be pretty sure that this change will take place – probably within a month. But as far as timing is concerned, common sense is essential, and if the nature of the job is such that many months are required before the client can leave, the degree is more likely to represent around a year, and the Moon will be a more reliable indicator of timing.

When dealing with the consultation horoscope, there is a very important point to consider – planets fall *backwards* through the houses as the Earth turns on its axis. Thus the Sun rises on the Ascendant and rises up into the 12th house. Planets fall from culmination on the MC and then into the 9th. This movement – which is contrary to what astrologers are accustomed to seeing with progressions – can be very descriptive of the client's situation. For example, when a planet is on the cusp of the 6th house in the consultation chart, it is actually on the point of moving into the 5th. This can be clearly seen on the Astrodial. This may for example reflect a person who at this point of his life is about to give up his job (6th house) so that he can concentrate on something creative or to have children (5th house).

Finally it is worth considering the phenomenon of *refranation*. This is the horary rule which states that 'perfection' will not be attained if a significator leaves the sign before the client's significator aspects it.

Let us assume that Libra is rising with Venus in, say, the middle of Leo, and the client asks for example if her partner will come back to her. One can safely assume that this will not happen if Mars (significator for the partner as ruler of the 7th) is in the last degrees of Sagittarius –

even though Venus is applying by trine to Mars. Mars will leave Sagittarius before the trine is made. The man is on his way to other pastures; no longer interested in a narcissistic relationship, he wants to get down to some serious work (Mars in Capricorn in the 2nd house).

I have seen refranation illustrated on several occasions. Sometimes an aspect is just at the point of being made and success seems sure – but suddenly new circumstances arise, as a significator changes sign and makes achievement of the goal impossible.

Cutting Through

The following example may serve to illustrate the value of the consultation horoscope in breaking through reserve and secrecy. Many people who go to therapists harbour fears and secrets which they never share with anybody. These secrets tend to absorb far too much energy. Sharing them with a consultant or therapist helps to liberate the energy tied up in them, bringing about a positive transformation.

This consultation horoscope did not reflect the birth horoscope very much, except for the fact that the horary Ascendant fell on the natal MC, emphasising the theme of career. The themes of secrecy and sexuality shown strongly in this chart were only indirectly reflected in the birth chart by Venus in the 12th square Saturn, and Pluto in the 7th (secret, guilt-ridden affairs). Normally far more surprising correlations can be expected, particularly with new variations of natal aspect patterns, Moon in same sign, Mercury–Sun pattern repeated, etc. The fact that there was a strong emphasis on Scorpio and the 8th house in the consultation chart showed an acute crisis out of context with the main themes of the client's life.

The major themes to look at are those shown by the Ascendant ruler and Moon. Now this was the period in November and December of 1987 when Mars conjuncted Pluto in Scorpio, a real power combination of great danger.

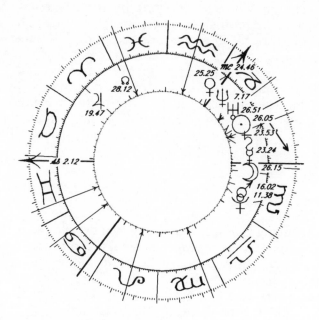

Chart 4.2: 18 Dec. 1987, 13.00 CPH

As many of my clients came in the early afternoon during
this period, Mars–Pluto fell in the 5th and 6th houses –
often 'intercepted', a factor which increased the secrecy
of the goings-on this combination represented. I was
actually getting rather used to themes connected with
secret affairs with employees (6th house theme – the
excitement!), or dangerous liaisons between mothers-in-
law and stepchildren (5th house theme); well there really
are no limits to the taboo drives and temptations connected
with this conjunction. My male clients at this time were
often men of great power and influence in secretive jobs,
banks or computer firms, who were involved in a sexual
liaison which really was a great threat to them.

In the case of the meeting shown in Chart 4.2, with the
Ascendant ruler Mercury, symbolising my client, applying
to a close conjunction with Saturn on the cusp of the
8th, it was not difficult to see that he was very worried

indeed. The question was – about what? A direct question would not provide the answer: with Mercury–Saturn the lips are tightly sealed. The 8th house represents many things, and one area much overlooked is the issue of security. People with planets in this house are anxious about losing security and try to insure themselves against catastrophe. Often then, they are involved with large firms, banks, pension schemes or large and powerful organisations which ensure immortality of a sort. And sure enough my client had been working in a bank for many years, had decided to resign in favour of another job that was lined up for him. Having dropped the one job, it turned out that the other job was no longer available. At the age of 50, how was he going to find work?

This story fits well with the astrological picture of anxiety about work as shown by the 6th house, and the anxiety about money and security as shown by the 8th. But with the extremely powerful picture of unpredictability as shown by Sun–Uranus in the 8th, together with Moon, Pluto and Mars in Scorpio, there was obviously a more acute factor that was worrying him. What was the significance of Venus culminating on the MC yet ruling two intercepted (and therefore secret) houses? I asked if he had been having (past tense because the Moon had passed both Pluto and Mars) an affair with someone at work, and was anxious about this. No. I asked if he had any anxiety about his health. At this point he became alert, asking if I could see anything. I certainly did not want to increase my client's anxiety, even though the 6th and 8th house patterns seemed disastrous, so I started talking generally about anxiety about death – the theme which was most clearly dominant in this chart.

At this point outside agencies came into play. The telephone company knocked on the door – somebody had been using a phone illegally in the building and they were trying to track the particular phone contact that had been used – not unlike my own detective process! This is of course the Mercury–Saturn theme (stealing information) reflected in the world outside. Old connections were broken and new connections made, and when I returned after ten minutes my client was feeling much more open. It turned out that while he had been in Zaîre on business (Sun–Uranus in Sagittarius – here Sun–Uranus had 'fallen' from the 9th – travel to the 8th – crisis) he had enjoyed the 'services' of a prostitute. What with publicity about Aids, especially in Africa, he was now convinced that he had contracted the disease. Interestingly a love affair would have been a 5th house issue, but prostitution was obviously hard work – a 6th house affair, and the emphasis on Scorpio showed perhaps the theme of darkest Africa and a black prostitute.

He had had an Aids test and now had to wait a whole month for the result. With 1 degree before the Sun hit Uranus, and also 1 degree before his significator Mercury hit Saturn, the astrologer may have been tempted to think that the news would be bad. Of course I said emphatically that he had not contracted the disease – no point in encouraging negative thoughts at this time, and anyway the Moon was void of course; according to the rules of horary, nothing would come of the matter. At the same time Venus would culminate on the MC in one month, and the Sun was translating the light by trine from Jupiter to Uranus, so there seemed to be a secure foundation for good news. But I was not sure.

Having brought the major anxiety into the open we could discuss remedies, and the consultation chart here clearly showed the value of confronting fear of death and disaster – both physical and professional. Sun–Uranus indicated an alternative approach which could lead to a profound change of consciousness. He ended up enrolling on an intense two-week meditation course where he specifically came to terms with the issue of death. The Aids test came up negative. He was considering taking up a more creative job – MC culminating on Venus – and had taken up painting again and had joined an avant-garde art group (probably symbolised by 5th house ruler Sun conjoining Uranus as ruler of the 11th).

And later a new job offer turned up connected with the administration of international aid – a Sun–Uranus in the 8th theme.

In this case the consultation horoscope gave me the courage to stick to themes which were of central importance to the client, but not particularly obvious in the birth chart. As far as the client was concerned the consultation had a strong cathartic effect, and thereby had a reassuring and healing function.

The supreme value of the consultation chart is in pinpointing themes in the birth chart which are relevant at that place and time for the client. An apparently weak aspect in the natal chart may be strongly emphasised in the horary, so the astrologer will know it is important. A little-understood configuration in the natal chart may be clarified by the consultation chart, and the astrologer is able to be far more accurate, and thereby gains credibility and trust.

Omens and Portents

We have learned that a horoscope cast for the moment of a question will reveal the past and present circumstances around the question, and give a pointer towards future development of the issue. Horary astrology is based on this premise. We can also clearly see that a chart cast for the arrival of a client will to a greater or lesser extent reflect the present circumstances of the client and even the whole life. Some of the most potent consultation charts occur when the client is delayed. Here Life itself conspires to synchronise the client's fate and the arrival chart in the most telling way.

In my personal travels – to astrological conferences for example – I have found that the simple enquiry concerning demonstration of the Astrodial is enough to constitute a consultation chart. It is often found that the innocent enquirer has a planet at a significant point on the Astrodial (for example on the Ascendant or MC) culminating at that very moment. The horoscope formed at the moment of enquiry will often reflect the enquirer's circumstances to an extraordinary degree. The Astrodial is most definitely an invasion of privacy. It is no accident that a particular individual comes with a particular enquiry at a particular moment.

To take this a step further let us imagine that you are sitting in a train and a person steps into your compartment and sits opposite you. This moment of entry will probably also constitute a consultation chart. If you do not talk to your fellow traveller, you will not find out if this hypothesis is true or not. I can, however, remember one particular instance when I put this to the test. It was an excellent time to try, because I knew that the exact square of the Moon to Pluto had just been formed. A lady had entered the carriage and we had fallen into conversation. Daily experience with horary astrology gives rise to an automatic awareness of what Ascendant is rising at a particular time, and I realised that Libra was rising with Pluto in the 2nd house square Moon in Aquarius in the 5th.

As the subject got around to astrology she showed an interest in her own horoscope, but I informed her that knowledge of her birth data was not necessary, as the actual conversation constituted a horoscope which would be relevant to her. She was naturally sceptical and asked me if I could guess what had just happened to her. Now Moon square Pluto is not the stuff of polite everyday conversations in trains as there is often a taboo and secret element about the situation particularly in connection with sexuality. Not the stuff to talk to fifty-year-old ladies about. Nevertheless I asked if she had perhaps just lost a large sum of money very recently – Moon–Pluto was exact and Pluto in the 2nd. She indeed had lost a considerable sum – unfortunately for her, but fortunately for the reputation of astrology. She didn't elaborate, and neither did I expect her to. Suddenly I had to change stations, and that was the last I saw of her – the last, that is, for six months.

The lady had seen my picture in another connection and found my telephone number, so now, six months on, she rang and made an appointment for a consultation. As I had imagined, the true story was really quite gruesome. This lady worked with integrating immigrants into society and had in this connection fallen in love with a young immigrant twenty years her junior and this had indeed led to an important sexual reawakening for her. She also had an adopted daughter who was twelve years younger than the man. The man became attracted to the daughter, and she to him, and a love affair ensued. It does not take much imagination to visualise the catastrophic results of this affair for my client, who in reality lost a daughter and a lover in one cruel blow, along with the considerable sum of money she had lent the man. All this was quite clearly reflected in Moon in Aquarius in the 5th (adopted daughter/foreigner) square Pluto.

It turned out that her own birth chart contained a similar Moon–Pluto pattern. An interesting detail was the presence of the Moon's North Node in Aquarius in conjunction with Uranus in her natal 5th house, which indicated something of the deeper karmic meaning of her adoption of the daughter and the explosive effects of untraditional love affairs.

Not only does this kind of event make train journeys more interesting, but life itself takes on quite a different tone. If you are aware of planetary patterns around you, then small 'irritations' in daily life become the source of fascination and education. Just observing the movement of a planet from one sign to another as reflected in daily life can be quite amusing. On the day Mars moved into Gemini in March 1989 – precisely square Mercury in Pisces – I found myself travelling into town to a party. There were many delays on the Underground train that evening and we had to wait in the train. Looking to my right I noticed a forty-year-old man in anorak and corduroy trousers, relaxed and sporty. Opposite him, another man in anorak and corduroy trousers, relaxed and sporty. Double-take: identical twins! Mars in Gemini. A young girl is in the other compartment with a large alsatian dog. She obviously doesn't like travelling alone on trains. The dog looks threatening. Another girl steps onto the train with an alsatian dog: yes, Mars in Gemini. Changing from train to bus, as I am getting in a woman complains bitterly to the driver that there is a rude man in the bus who should be thrown off. Mars in Gemini. What kind of party was it? Argumentative – with lots of gossip.

This is the month when two films are competing for first place in the ratings in the USA – one is *Rainman* and the other *Twins* – both about brothers, who first discover each other's existence later in adult life. In the same month the film *Dead Ringers* is released; based on a true story with Jeremy Irons playing the role of two identical twins who share the same mistress and are found dead in their apartment under mysterious circmstances. The media are simply wonderful reflectors of planetary influences. This is something that Dennis Elwell points out in his book *The Cosmic Loom*:

> If you watch world events from month to month or year to year, as they coincide with the various types of planetary configurations, you feel as if you are in a theatre where the spotlight is turned now here, now there. It is as if the cosmos is repeatedly crying, 'Look!' Often it seems that astrology points to a 'tabloid reality' in which events are graded according to their degree of impact on public consciousness rather than any statistical yardstick.

Life's events will tend to reflect planetary positions. It is very possible that those who work closely with astrology will actually experience this more than people who don't. There are just not enough twins to go round to sit next to people in trains when Mars moves into Gemini for example. To some extent you can choose the code through which life will talk to you, and for astrologers it is the planets. (For statisticians it is numbers, and probably they shouldn't mix!) Obviously events can be seen as envoys for planets, just as planets can be seen as envoys for events. It would not be a bad assumption to imagine that there was a Mars in Gemini type influence for example, should you happen to meet aggression on a bus, and possibly you could apply this in some other area. Perhaps you are actually thinking about your own brother with annoyance when you experience aggression on a bus – a kind of correlating activity. These events will mean something to you, and you can learn from them. This is the lateral landscape of Uranus and the world of astrology so well described in Dennis Elwell's book.

It is also this kind of thinking that gives significance to the world of omens and portents. Any event happening within your field of experience will actually be a reflection of your state of mind at that particular moment. Just as a horary chart cast for a question will reflect the question and its resolution, so will events strive to form a significant mandala around you. If you are going around with a question in your head, then life will be busy ordering itself to give you an answer. Many people discover this, but not everybody can handle it. Misinterpreting the totality of the field of the mind, some people are gripped by fear and uncertainty, or by delusions of grandeur or megalomania. Grasping half the truth can lead to severe paranoia or mental disturbance, and the wards of mental hospitals have their share of people trying to convince personnel in white aprons about the many and varied signs they have personally been vouchsafed by God. I find that snippets of conversation as people pass by, comments heard sychronistically on the radio and many other things can have a direct bearing on a particular problem I have at a particular moment. And why not? All things arise sychronised with the planetary forces of the moment, and as such bear a relation to each other.

Some omens hit you on the head with the subtlety of a sledgehammer, others are more refined. If for example you were discussing the wisdom of a deep-sea diving trip with an unreliable daredevil friend, and an ambulance went by with sirens blaring as he was trying to assure you that there was no real danger involved, then there would hardly be a need to cast a horary chart for the question. If you were driving in a car thinking seriously about whether to continue with a relationship or drop it completely and you drove past a building being demolished, then the symbolism in itself would be enough to suggest that the relationship was in ruins and should be eliminated without sentiment in true Pluto style.

Of course this kind of attention to omens is not new, and books do exist interpreting omens just as there are books of dream interpretation. Birds play a very significant role as far as omens and portents are concerned – especially in old cultures as evidenced for example by Carlos Castaneda's books concerning the teachings of Don Juan.

The crow is definitely a Saturn bird, and its cawing seems often like an admonition to get down to hard work, its flight seemingly filled with intent and purpose, each wingbeat filled with effort and struggle. The crow demands attention and respect and warns of hard work ahead. One woman who had left her home for the weekend to attend one of my courses – which included material on omens and portents – discovered on her return that a pair of ravens had started building a nest in her chimney. It was an old country cottage with a very large chimney, and the ravens were actually constructing the nest at the bottom of her chimney, almost in the living room. What could this mean? – she asked. At the same time she asked me about a horary chart she had made asking whether she should start working as a professional astrologer to supplement her income. No need to cast the horary here. The ravens symbolise the need to work hard, and their nest-building almost in her living room might well indicate that working from home will be lucrative. Ravens are well-known for their ability to communicate and imitate human speech – giving consultations, and also for their associations with hoarding valuables and jewellery. In other words there is a promise of financial reward here.

The pigeon or dove is a Venus bird, its flight effortless and full of grace and its cooing full of sweetness and reassurance – it promises harmony and peace, and of course has been collectively seen as a harbinger of peace and forgiveness since the time of Noah. Passing a dead pigeon in the gutter does not bode well if matters of the heart are on the mind, whereas two doves landing in a tree would be a good sign. Sparrows seem to be Moon–Mercury birds to me; homebodies, flashing through the air like stray ideas, birds as thoughts. The owl has a bad reputation forewarning family problems. I can remember a time when a particular owl would fly in front of my car on my journey home during a period when transiting Pluto was opposing my Moon: a major restructuring time.

And then there are birds of a more mechanical nature – jet aircraft flying through the ether, symbolising Uranus, excitement and sudden and imminent change. Helicopters are quite different and much more threatening with a stronger suggestion of Pluto carrying the threat of destruction or spying. Generally speaking traffic noise shows the pervading influence of Pluto in everyday life, as the combustion chamber explosions (Uranus) are dampened and exhaust gases expelled (Pluto).

With this plethora of information around us the astrologer uses the horoscope as a crutch, resorting to the computer or ephemeris to understand things which are obvious to the person who is a keen student of omens and portents, for whom Nature is teacher. One could imagine that this is the kind of wisdom available to shamans, witch-doctors and other mystics, who have no need to clutter their minds with figures and planetary orbits. Still, in the country of the blind, the astrologer is a one-eyed man.

The concept of omens extends, of course, into interpretation of the consultation chart. For example, I find Mercury square Pluto a very dangerous aspect in the consultation. Something unforseen happens with the tape or the tape recorder so often with this aspect, that I take special precautions to ensure that the recording is functioning. When a client rings to tell me that there is nothing on the tape, I must take my share of the blame. Yet I also know that this also suggests an area in the person's life

which they do not want to hear or communicate about.
Here are a couple of variations on the Mercury–Pluto
theme:

On one occasion the phone rang just as I sat down
with the client. It was the police who informed me that
they were in possession of some letters addressed to me.
It turned out that a thief had been apprehended who
had been coming into our centre and stealing letters.
This was a powerful omen for my client – and it struck
me how much it related to my client's chart (4.3), who had
Moon–Mercury opposition Uranus–Pluto from the 2nd to
the 8th (using Koch – I tend to look at both Koch and
Placidus). What information was being kept from him?

I did not find out what information was being concealed
or distorted – Mercury–Pluto is very secretive – but
I learned how he was indoctrinated by his mother's
martyrdom against his father. He had followed his father's
footsteps in the army, but dropped out and wanted to be a

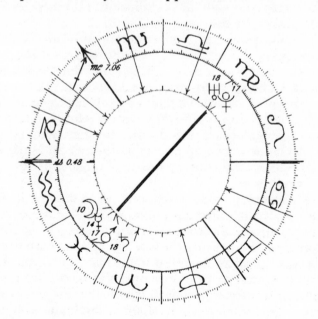

Chart 4.3: Client

musician: obviously the right choice here. One interesting point was that his father came from one of the oldest aristocratic families in the country, and he had lost the whole family estate through a bankruptcy. To lose the family fortune was quite clearly the son's karma here.

On another occasion there was a more concrete loss of information. The client was also born in 1966, but this time with Mars, Uranus and Pluto in the 3rd house opposite Saturn in the 9th – hence the definite emphasis on communication. When putting the kettle on to make her a cup of tea, the fuse blew and the analysis that I had written – but not stored – on my computer was lost for ever. This related strongly to actions in her own life. She had totally cut off and refused to communicate with her father, because he had had a mental breakdown. The pain of his fall from grace had caused her to cauterise a whole area of her mind. With her stellium in Virgo in the 3rd (information), and the associations with electronics and sudden loss (Uranus–Pluto), my word-processing system just about had to short-circuit!

Mercury–Saturn will also show problems with communication. On one occasion I missed the train on the way to work (Mercury–Saturn), and encountered my client on the way home again from my office. It turned out that she was a writer who had a Mercury–Saturn square in her natal chart, and after forty years of her life Mercury had progressed retrograde and was now squaring Saturn yet again. Her problem was writer's block, and lack of confidence about her book which was about the silent inner world of incest victims.

The same day, with the Mercury square Saturn still active, my next client rang one and a half hours *before* our appointment to say that she had already arrived at the station, and asking if it was all right to take the bus that was waiting and arrive early. I told her it was and to get off at the fourth stop. But after ringing off, it occurred to me that something was bound to go wrong considering Mercury–Saturn's reputation for misunderstandings, so I walked down to the main road. Sure enough, the bus sailed past the bus stop without stopping. I set off doggedly on foot after the bus, thinking that she would probably get off at the next stop, and when the bus stopped about 300 metres away, I observed a red blob emerging – my client. Unfortunately she started walking *away* from me, and some time elapsed before she hesitated and looking round caught sight of me. Somewhat delayed then, our first meeting took place on the pavement about half a mile from my office, just as had happened with my earlier client. Strange!

What was even more striking here was that Uranus had just moved retrograde at 26°43′ Sagittarius, and my client's Moon was at 26°46′ Sagittarius. Now the astrologer clearly is symbolised by Uranus, I could not help being struck by the fact that the woman came 'too early', and both passed me on the bus *and* walked away from me when she got off. It was too early to meet Uranus which had not quite reached her Moon, and indeed nine months would go by before Uranus came to make the first exact conjunction with her Moon.

There is a strong symbolic parallel here. Translated into real terms, this woman was extremely restless in her marriage and desperate for change and excitement. Yet she had decided not to do anything drastic and to try to stick things out. Obviously, if she felt like this before Uranus conjuncted her Moon, it was unlikely that her stable home life would survive the coming three conjunctions of Uranus – and indeed after nine months she moved away from her husband and tried to make a go of her life alone. Experience shows that the condition, mood and actions of the astrologer prior to the consultation can often be interpreted as part of the consultation mandala.

Omens can be very humorous. I was having a regular series of powerful psychological sessions with one woman who had Mars–Pluto rising in Leo, and one day she turned up with her friend – a private student of mine – who also had a heavy Pluto influence. Interestingly the Moon was in Gemini, and I have often experienced two people coming together with this mutable sign horary influence. The appointment was at 11.00 a.m. and the doorbell rang promptly. Yet when I opened the door I found the postman standing there instead with a parcel. It contained a wriggling mass of worms – compost worms which my wife had ordered for the garden. At the same time the two ladies walked up the drive. Well Pluto can be a real can of worms – but the omen is good, and shows that useless clutter and waste is about to be transformed and converted to useful compost to enable future growth – definitely a positive Pluto influence.

The secret of prediction lies in this awareness of the synchronicity of events, coupled with a certain amount of common sense. My examples here are but the clumsy beginnings of a study which could take a whole lifetime. In past cultures there were people whose ability to read omens and combine it with a philosophical system was legendary. In Europe there was for example Nostradamus, who lived quite humbly and was visited by Kings. Another such sage was Shao Yung (born in China in AD 1011), who based his predictions on the eight trigrams of the *I Ching*.

It is unlikely that we will be able to emulate the feats, of the great seers of the past. Yet through combining a simple knowledge of planetary positions and aspects with trained powers of observation we can at least sharpen our consciousness – perhaps even up to the point of being able to do without the horoscope – under some circumstances.

Our Outer Skins

Transitory daily influences while we are on the move will certainly tend to reflect our inner psychic state. Yet the objects which daily surround us and which are an expression of our taste and character will reflect circumstances in our life in even greater depth. The state of our houses and cars in particular will reflect developments, problems and changes in our circumstances and give a hint of necessary steps to be taken. So let us look at omens in action.

On one occasion I was called upon to introduce astrology to a group of sceptical businessmen at an annual get-together. A guinea-pig had been chosen, a manager of a printing firm, on whose horoscope I had to comment. Fate smiled on me that night because the man had the Moon in Taurus conjunct the MC. Fate was, however, not smiling on him: transiting Pluto was precisely opposite his Moon. The astrologer who leans towards the psychological may have been tempted to ask the businessman if he was going through an extremely difficult emotional crisis; but, in front of twelve slightly tipsy business acquaintances, it is unlikely that the guinea-pig will admit to any weaknesses. I felt that a slightly sneaky approach was called for. I started by asking him whether his toilet or sink was blocked. To general consternation and amusement it turned out that this was in fact the case. One sceptic suggested that I had

Chart 4.4: Blocked toilets

had a lucky break, as everybody's toilet blocks once in a while. Ah, yes, I said, but with astrology you can tell *when* your toilet will be blocked. Ascertaining where the sceptic's Moon was I correctly guessed when his toilet had last suffered from this problem.

Transiting Pluto aspects to the Moon really do tend to cause blockages on many levels, and I chose to go for the most banal because it is the easiest to verify. I also asked the manager if he had a cellar in his house, which he confirmed. Had a problem with damp suddenly arisen in the cellar (Pluto over the IC)? Well, yes, but only because water had been running down from an unrepaired gutter in the roof, he said defensively. Problems with the roof in the house are an MC issue (here the Moon), problems with the cellar an IC issue.

Having isolated basic material problems it was easy then to introduce more personal questions about the mother (Moon) who, it turned out, was still actively involved in the running of the firm at the age of 70 (represented here by Moon in Taurus conjunct the MC). Obviously it was necessary to send his mother into retirement (Pluto opposition Moon) if he wanted future growth to take place. This would also mean a strong emotional development for the man, whose wife was none too glad about the central role that the man's mother still had in his life.

Issues of house and car maintenance have much to say about changes in our life. Work being done, or events occurring under people's feet will symbolise a process of emotional transformation for the person concerned. This could be the clearing out of a cellar, or working on the foundations of the house. For someone living in a flat problems connected with alcohol, drug-misuse, deaths or arguments in the flat downstairs could be a reflection of Neptune or Pluto influences in the 4th house of their own chart. So if you visit someone who is in the process of renovating their cellar you know that this parallels some expansion of their unconscious which may also be connected with an emotional trauma. You may wish to ask them about their relationship to their mother, or about the mother's health (which may be undergoing a transformation), or about other emotionally charged matters.

If on the other hand they are clearing out the attic, it is more likely that they are considering some change or expansion of their job or status. Perhaps there are changes in the father's situation here, or general parental upheaval. It depends of course on the exact circumstances. A leak in the roof could be a Neptune influence: perhaps there is disappointment or dissatisfaction with the career, perhaps clarification of goals is necessary. Should something happen to the TV aerial then this would be a Uranian symbol, perhaps indicating sudden and unforeseen developments, travel, or sudden breaks, etc. A roof collapse could indicate being fired or sudden business shock. Alteration to the façade or windows of the house will be connected to the Ascendant–Descendant axis and may also correspond to partnership upheaval and changes in personal appearance – and with windows in particular there will be a new way of looking at things. The reader is advised *not* to take my word for this. Look at your own experiences in these matters concerning, say, building alterations, and make your own judgement. New dimensions of life-experience arise!

It pays to listen very closely to offhand remarks, especially in the consultation, which give a clue to developments in hidden areas of a person's nature. Problems in the central heating system due to overheating or high pressure could easily symbolise repressed anger reaching a danger level – perhaps shown by a Mars–Uranus conjunction in a water sign. Rats under the floorboards could indicate morbid thoughts and phobias which need to be dealt with – a Mercury–Neptune aspect perhaps. When a fire breaks out in a person's home, it is clear that more gentle warnings have already been ignored. A fire could show passions ignored too long, and is a general indication that some drastic change needs to be contemplated.

The personal horoscope will actually show certain predispositions to problems in the home, with planets in the

4th house and in the 10th showing what can come up from below, or down from above respectively. Moon–Pluto and Mars–Pluto aspects could indicate blockage – from the sewage system to problems with constipation or fertility in the body. Mercury–Pluto could show a general disposition to have the bicycle stolen, the postman bitten by the dog, problems with the car (particularly the exhaust system) or difficult neighbours. Mars–Uranus could indicate electrical short-circuits, problems with starting the car, etc. There are innumerable possibilities, yet each problem will carry a planetary signature which can be successfully applied symbolically to another area of the life.

So-called practical problems and irritations in daily life are often the Cosmos's way of gently nudging the individual to pay attention. It is probable that the more attention you pay, the more gently you will be nudged. When the nudge becomes a heavy blow – in the case of a serious accident or illness – it seems likely that not enough attention has been paid, in some cases at least. One young woman I know managed to write off two cars before the age of 20. With Mars, Pluto and Uranus in the 3rd house we can recognise the planetary signature. But this combination of planets also indicates dangerously repressed aggressions, which she gave vent to in the privacy of her car by swearing at other drivers, insisting on the right of way and generally making sure that she was not going to be taken for the weaker sex (Mars–Pluto). Her accidents, from which she escaped both times without injury, were not acts of Fate, but rather events evoked by her own unconscious as a message of compassion.

Houses as Doors

Awareness of the subtleties and shifts of ever-changing atmosphere and tone reveals a world pregnant with meaning and possibility, a world of expressions and actions of archetypal power and significance. Focus of attention on any particular event, quirk or foible sucks the awareness into a vortex in whose depths lies the secret of human fate and destiny. Through the houses in the horoscope, through the crack in the human façade or the careless omission in a sentence is revealed a hidden world which when brought to the surface can enrich understanding of the individual.

This magic world is paralleled by new computer techniques which convert mathematical formulae into images, which when zoomed in upon form new images in a constant and infinite inner expansion – the world of *fractals*. A banal image is the outer shell concealing another image which is more complex, concealing an image which is more complex, and so on *ad infinitum*.

The houses of the horoscope are also a kind of fractal world in which each event or image is a door opening onto a deeper event or image until the very core of the personal psyche is accessed. In the consultation process it often pays to concentrate attention initially on comparatively banal areas of experience, and then to probe progressively deeper. Thus, instead of coming with a ready-processed psychological formula the astrologer can guide the client through each fractal door in an easily digestible process.

It is generally true that a Venus–Saturn conjunction will give the experience of rejection in love – in early life, at least – and a subsequent defensive attitude to relationships. Should the astrologer inform the client of this, the client would probably confirm the diagnosis with a resigned sigh, no matter which house the conjunction was to be found in. A more rewarding approach, however, would be to identify the precise earthly manifestation of the aspect. Let us suppose it was in the 6th house of a female client. Now there are several areas where rejection would be experienced. In the work environment the client might experience that colleagues give her the cold shoulder, or that an older employee makes her life difficult day in, day out.

The task of the astrologer is to show the client how this present-day experience is actually evoked by a behaviour rooted in an earlier experience. The astrologer could try to guess what this might be or ask an intelligent question. Perhaps as a child her mother expected her to take responsibility for a younger sister, so that instead of going out to enjoy herself she was forced to stay at home doing household tasks. Thus an attitude of resentment might have arisen in connection with work which will be felt by the people she works with in the future. By leading the client to make the connection from the childhood area to the adult area, a healing process is started which will enable the client to change her programming.

Events from the childhood and family relationships can be identified reasonably easily in the horoscope, but they are only really important in so far as they are responsible for experiences here and now. It is the present situation that is important – not the past. But the past is useful for understanding the present. In identifying past patterns it is important to see how family members influenced the client's character. Obviously the Sun and Moon are extremely important and will show how an individual experiences the mother and father. A description of the Sun and its aspects, or the Moon and its aspects, will generally be recognised by the client as a good description of the father and mother respectively. Mars and Venus, however, must not be forgotten as symbols in their own right for brothers and sisters respectively in the horoscope. Siblings play an important and underestimated role in the development of character. Mercury, too, can symbolise a brother or a sister. A family is a complete unit in itself, and if there is anything special about one part of that unit – a mentally ill brother for example – then it can be identified in the client's horoscope as an area of imbalance which will also affect other areas of the life.

Thus, when dealing with a taboo and sensitive issue like a Mars–Pluto square in the horoscope it can be quite effective to approach the aspect through the brother, if there is one. Often with this aspect there are half-brothers, adopted brothers or seriously disturbed brothers – or at least an alienation from the brother. It is not uncommon for a person to cut off personal connections with a brother.

And there is generally a good reason for it. Questioning about childhood may reveal that the client was literally terrorised by the brother. The Mars–Pluto aspect here would indicate the incredible reserves of will-power that the client had to summon up just to survive. Obviously this means that the person would develop the ability to survive in quite extreme situations, and this can be quite useful. But on the other hand it might also show a tendency to get involved in power battles and confrontations – especially with men – which may cause misery and suffering later on.

It might turn out that a man with a Venus–Uranus contact had a sister whom he only saw rarely because she went to boarding school in a foreign country. His experience of women might then be connected with sudden partings and reunions, long-distance travel and a general atmosphere of excitement. This might explain possible problems in existing relationships because of restlessness or boredom. Mercury–Saturn in the 8th house might indicate a trauma connected to the death of a pet which could explain present unwillingness to establish close bonds. It might also indicate a brother who told lies with the result that the client has learned to be very secretive, thus causing communication problems in later relationships.

Sometimes the influences of the houses comes through in a classic manner. I remember a father, who had Sun in Pisces in the 5th house opposite Neptune in the 11th, who was desperately unhappy because his son was involved with drugs. He asked how he could help his son. Yet it turned out that this son was one of many children the father had had with several different women. In other words his own irresponsible attitude to fatherhood and love affairs (Sun in Pisces in the 5th – opposition Neptune) returned to haunt him in the form of a son who – in this case – was wanted by the police. He could have helped his son by reforming his own character – he also had been involved in criminality and violence. While in transit through an airport, this man was injured when a maintenance engineer accidentally dropped a hammer on his head, with the result that he suffered from persistent headaches later on. This was a very clear expression of Mars in the 9th (airport hammer) square his Pluto in the 7th. As I had heard many stories about this person's maltreatment of others, it occurred to me that the mechanic was merely acting out the collective wish of many people who had been this man's victims.

There are countless variations of planetary effects in different houses, but it is good training to deal with the concrete manifestations. It is after all comparatively easy to describe the psychological effects of planetary aspects divorced from their house positions, and more demanding to identify mundane effects. Yet by approaching these 'surface issues' there is a tangible area for the client to work on and transform. In this sense there is no such thing as 'superficial' – everything has value as a handle on the unconscious.

5

The Practice

The truth is that we are all players in a Marionette comedy.
The most important thing in a Marionette comedy, my
children, is to keep the Author's Idea clear. *Seven Gothic Tales*
– Karen Blixen (Isak Dinesen)

Astrotherapy

Astrology offers a system not based on any particular
individual and later made into dogma by his or her
followers. The most important ingredient, after an understanding of the horoscope, is *attention*. As such, astrological therapy can learn a lot from gestalt therapy, which
is a system very much based on what is going on here-and-
now in the consultation. Gestalt therapy looks for answers
to problems in the behaviour of clients at each particular
moment – just as the astrologer sees a question or the
whole of the life reflected in the horoscope for a particular
moment. It is not so much a question of what happened
in the past as how the past is still affecting the present
through unconscious behaviour. These unconscious and
therefore distorted processes deprive us of energy and
diminish our awareness and enjoyment of the present.
Furthermore we protect ourselves from present intensity
by thinking constantly about the future or rationalising
about the past. This leads to feelings of boredom and
meaninglessness in the present.

Through horary techniques combined with the birth

chart it is possible to give the client valuable insight into past conditioning factors, the present situation and future trends. But the possibility also arises to initiate changes in the client here-and-now which will exert a lasting positive influence. It might here be worth quoting the Chinese book of wisdom, the *I Ching* which, when talking about influence in hexagram 61 (Inner Truth) says:

> One must first rid oneself of all prejudice and, so to speak, let the psyche of the other person act on one without restraint. Then one will establish contact with him, understand and gain power over him. When the door has thus been opened, the force of one's personality will influence him.

In other words it is important to be free of preconceptions and prejudice, and open to what the client is experiencing. No one can explain the personal horoscope better than the client, whose words are like pearls to be treasured and stored. In the therapeutic process it pays dividends simply to make the client aware of his words. Explanations are best kept to a minimum – far better to draw out the explanation from the client himself through astute questioning. Instead of giving solutions it might pay to ask clients themselves to come with proposals.

Plato maintained that the best way of teaching his students was to ask them questions. This forced them to think, and thinking independently gave them wisdom. Intelligent questioning can evoke an understanding of complex areas of the chart, whereas astrological explanations and rationalisations tend to evoke resistance in the client. For example, a person with Sun and Moon in Virgo once complained to me about how lazy her husband was. Resisting the temptation to give a classical interpretation of Virgo perfectionism I chose to let the awareness arise spontaneously in the client:

Client: He never does any work in the home.
Astrologer: You mean to say that he never, ever washes the dishes? [*Specifying*]
C: Well yes he does, but he never does them properly.

A: What do *you* do when you discover he hasn't done the dishes properly?

C: Well I have to clear up after him.

A: So he is prepared to work in the home, but he cannot live up to your standards. Is that right?

C: Yes. If I want something to be done properly, I have to do it myself.

A: Can you see why you end up doing all the work?

The astrologer has an advantage over the psychologist here, because he can recognise the astrological signature for the problem immediately. But it is not enough for the astrologer to recognise the astrological pattern: he has to make the client aware of it in a down-to-earth way. It is important when using questions that the astrologer must know the answer, he must know what he is driving at. As the consultation progresses the client has the strong feeling that the astrologer knows the answers to the questions in advance. This can be quite humorous, keeps the client very awake, and ensures that the answers are as honest as possible.

The phrasing of questions is of paramount importance, and where possible the word 'Why?' should be completely avoided. Rationalisations and intellectualisations are of no real use. Much more to the point is the question 'How', because this leads to a description of actions, which can subsequently be modified. A man with a Venus–Saturn aspect complaining that his wife is frigid might come along with many explanations as to why. But the astrologer is more interested in *how* the man himself invokes frigidity in the wife:

Client: My wife is simply not interested in sex.

Astrologer: How do you know? [*A very useful question.*]

C: Well she won't let me touch her in bed.

A: How do you react to this?

C: Well, I don't like it!

A: How do you show this?

C: Well I turn away and don't talk to her.

In other words he ends up rejecting her. Whose rejection came first prior to this situation? The astrologer might then go on to relate this concrete behaviour to the past and question him about his earlier experience of rejection from women (the mother for example) – women who turned away from him and ignored him – until it dawns upon the man that his wife might want sex, but does not want sex devoid of love and vulnerability.

Gestalt therapy deals with so-called surface issues and opens the fractal gate into the deep unconscious just as astrology does through the houses. Dealing with material and concrete issues avoids an important pitfall, so often found in astrology. This is the division of astrology into the esoteric and the exoteric, the spiritual and the material, the body and the mind. This is a mere continuation of the 2,000-year-old dichotomy of polarity from the Piscean Age and leads to all kinds of negative projections and spiritual arrogance. Gestalt is the psychological equivalent of atomic physics – body and mind are One just as matter and energy are different expressions of one force.

Quantum physics theorises that matter is energy in extremely condensed form, planets and stars being areas of space where energy is tightly packed, or vibrating at a different level. In the horoscope physical manifestation is intimately linked to spiritual energy. Money is the fine concentrate of personal worth and action (2nd house), and orgasm the ultimate expression of concentrated feelings and potency (8th house). Material realities provide the key to the soul and character. It's no use aspiring to spiritual goals if you ignore damp in your cellar for example, because this damp will represent unfinished emotional issues which have been ignored and stand in the way of spiritual development. Similarly it is the actions and experiences of individuals which are a testimony to their inner thoughts and feelings. 'By their fruits you shall know them.' Actions and events are the final manifestation of character.

The consultation is a profound encounter between two identities which interreact. The meeting-point between astrologer and client is consciousness of the moment. At this point of time and space filled with consciousness, everything is possible. In the emptiness of the ever-extending present exists free will, and the possibility of changing that part of the personal fate which is based on conditioned responses, and accepting other areas of fate based on personal karma. In modern science it has been shown that the consciousness of the experimenter affects the results of the experiment, and in the same way the client can through consciousness regain control of his or her fate. But first the client must take responsibility for the circumstances he is in. It is the astrologer's job to draw the necessary parallels between fate and character, so that the client can take the first steps to altering negative character traits and steering the ship of karma.

The Client

In this section I would like to take a look at one such consultation which to some extent reflects the successful use of the consultation chart in combination with the birth chart. My client – Susan – is married to the gentleman who received a three-year prison sentence in Sweden mentioned earlier. Indeed she chose to marry him while he was in gaol – a very unusual course of action reflected by her very unusual horoscope. She is after all born in 1965 at the time of the Uranus–Pluto conjunction in Virgo opposition Saturn, which in her case is personalised because her Moon conjoins Pluto and Uranus. I am very grateful to her for allowing a transcript of our consultation to be used in this book.

On arrival she makes an impact, her black and white striped stockings for example, already indicating the strong Pluto theme in her chart. She is strongly non-conformist in appearance. She arrives ten minutes late, which brings the fast-moving Taurus Ascendant to 29 degrees Taurus – right on the star Alcyone, known as the 'Weeping Sisters', which has a reputation for

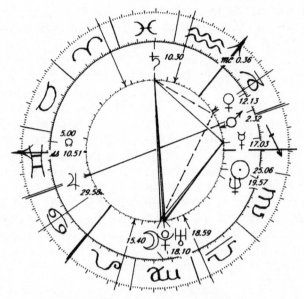

Chart 5.1   *The Birth Chart: Susan-17/11/1965. 16.35. Copenhagen*

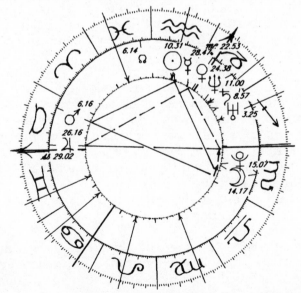

Chart 5.2   *The Consultation Chart: 30/01/1989. 11.10. Copenhagen*

unhappiness and tearfulness. The last degree rising suggests also imminent change – Gemini will soon exert a major influence.

She has come at the time of an imminent Moon–Pluto conjunction reflecting her own birth conjunction. The Sun is also applying to a square to Pluto. Obviously she is in crisis and it will not get easier. The one degree orb from the Moon to Pluto, and the imminent Ascendant change show a radical new situation arising within a month. At the same time the retrograde Mercury in the 10th is about to conjoin Venus direct in exact time to Jupiter–this represents a career opportunity. Mars, ruler of the horary 7th is intercepted in detriment in the 12th. This could not be worse and indicates quite clearly the confinement – and the character – of her husband. I ascertain from Susan that he has been transferred from a closed to an open prison but is not yet permitted to leave Sweden.

A: I can see a situation which is both good and bad – good in regard to future plans and possibilities, bad as far as your emotional situation is concerned. There is a career opportunity – something you have set in motion, some people you have been in contact with and perhaps have forgotten (Mercury retrograde), which will turn up trumps . . . an excellent opportunity is coming. This will really improve your economic situation. It has to do with your personal goals and career possibilities – practical things which bring good fortune. [*These comments are based on the ruling planet Venus in Capricorn in the 10th conjoining Mercury ruler of the 2nd and 6th and trining Jupiter*]. The difficult area is emotional – you are really in a crisis now. This is basically concerned with where you can settle, where you belong. It's really a question of clearing out.

S: Clearing out?

A: Yes. Perhaps I can use a symbol. [Here I show Susan a plant which my wife has just pruned the previous evening which is already looking beautiful and healthy after the dead leaves have been removed. Simultaneously I recall that council workers came round that very morning and cut the top branches of a tree in our garden which was getting entangled in the electricity lines. Rich symbolism for a Moon–Pluto day, and not irrelevant for my client's Moon–Pluto conjunction with Uranus, with its short-circuiting tendencies].

    You need to cut some things away. And it is quite clear that is really difficult for you at the moment to find your foundations. . . .

S: [Very spontaneously]. Yes!

A: [Continuing] . . . a strong psychological cleaning-out process is required, but the result will be good. [I know that her husband has been acting extremely badly – with Mars ruling the horary Descendant, in detriment in the 12th, and with the Moon (representing the client) in fall in Scorpio having opposed this Mars, their situation appears absolutely hopeless.] If I may comment on the cause of your emotional crisis. . . I see an extremely unpleasant conflict situation with your husband. This has to do with some of his secrets [Mars in 12th], and I believe there have been some exhausting arguments and battles of the will. [Client nods.] And if I were asked to pass judgement on the situation then I would have to say that his actions have been dishonest [client nods], and that you have every reason to be mad. He is not shown in a good light here [Mars in Taurus tends to be sensual, materialistic and sexually fixated, in horary at least], because of his lack of ability to control his desires. [Mars opposing Pluto showing a compulsive quality.] I get an impression that he is very selfishly independent and cannot see any need to compromise. Whereas you are shown in another light – with a desire to attain something in your life, serious and responsible, believe it or not . . . [ruler of Ascendant in Capricorn].

S: [Laughter]

A: . . . as a person who would like to have your life under control. And you will succeed in this. So the inner process now can be likened to a spring-cleaning. You will gain a deep insight into yourself, indeed you may feel a growing need to work with psychology or other deep issues in some way.

S: Hmm! [Agreeing]

Ten minutes have passed, and the client has only said a few words. It has been a one-sided show, so now it is time for a little ping-pong.

A: Now it's your turn!

S: Well, what you say fits really well . . . [laughs].

All my comments up to this point have been based entirely on the consultation horoscope. I can see they have made an impact, which in turn results in a very open attitude of mind in my client. We can now get down to the main issues without time-wasting or intellectual sparring. At this point we go into detail about career opportunities shown so clearly in the consultation chart. For the sake of brevity I will leave this section out, as I would like to concentrate mostly here on how Susan's parents had influenced her emotional development. The following section deals briefly with the dilemma Susan has in regarding her husband. Emotionally she was finished with him, but she had not quite come to terms with this yet.

The Husband – and Neptune

It turns out that her husband is actually expecting a child with another woman, and is involved in a relationship with yet another. If Susan comes back, he will apparently be prepared to give up this third woman. Well, big deal. Mars in Taurus has little dignity here!

A: How do you feel about this?

S: I don't want to go back . . . yet at the same time there are so many feelings. When I was with him before Christmas I reacted violently when I found out about the child . . . I felt so strongly that it should have been me and him that had the child . . . I was incredibly upset [note the horary Moon–Pluto conjunction, but also natal Moon–Pluto in the 5th]. I was really disappointed that he had not told me, and had lied to me about it. I found out about it through someone else. After that I refused to compromise [voice hardens] . . . I said 'No way' . . . I just don't have the energy to handle this confusion.

Understandably, Susan can't forgive the lies and unfaithfulness of her husband, yet.

S: . . . but I feel guilty about leaving him. When he was moved from a closed gaol to the open prison I simply couldn't take it any more, couldn't take Stockholm any more after one and a half years.

A: When he was in closed prison your relationship functioned well, and when he was in an open prison there were problems?

S: Yes, then the problems arose . . . [resigned].

A: How?

S: I guess it was because of me. I couldn't manage . . . I was in a period when I started to drink and our communication was really bad and foggy. He couldn't drink where he was . . . we each had a different state of mind . . . we just pulled each other to pieces. Finally we just couldn't talk together at all . . . I sat down every day and drank and drank and drank.

Well, the plot thickens. Here we see her natal Sun–Neptune conjunction intercepted in the 6th (partner's 12th . . . partner in gaol; a pattern confirmed by 7th house ruler in the horary 12th!). She has found the perfect projection for her own problems in her gaoled husband who is a musician and drug-dealer, and practises yoga.

The trick now is to get her to see this. This is going to relate to her father in some way. During the rest of the consultation I angle slowly in this direction.

The Karmic Plot

A: Have you stopped drinking now?

S: Yes . . . I feel I have. But clearly the tendency is there. It doesn't take much before I sit down again and . . . choose drink to get away.

A: Get away from what?

S: From the things I can't handle.

A: What can't you handle?

S: That there is no love [soft] . . . no security.

A: No love from whom?

S: Maybe from my husband.

A: Maybe? [Pause] Or from ..?

S: From myself.

A: To whom?

S: To my husband . . . I don't know.

A: You are sorry that there is no love or security.

S: – and understanding, perhaps.

Well this does not come easily with the Moon and Mercury in the natal chart under such pressure from the outer planets The 1989 Saturn–Neptune conjunction on her Venus now demands development through strength and isolation.

What is coming out at this point in the consultation is the Moon–Pluto–Uranus conjunction which opposes Saturn and squares Mercury in her birth chart. This will relate to her mother in some way. The Sun–Moon polarity in her chart can now also be clearly seen. I explain in some detail how her upbringing may actually make her unconsciously choose difficult emotional conditions. Susan confirms this by telling of a recent nightmare experience she has had with a room-mate who was at least partially psychotic – an experience which again echoes the Moon's placement in her horoscope. Susan was wise enough to see this experience as a reflection of the less palatable side of her own nature.

S: I learned a lot about myself.

A: For example?

S: [Sighs deeply] Egoism and all the things that come up in oneself like hate, slyness . . .

A: [Interrupting] Slyness? What slyness?

S: When I experienced her doing something completely crazy like putting catfood in my food – I am vegetarian – I asked myself why, and would I do it. And yes, I could do it . . . do bad things . . . at least when I was a child.

A: Under what circumstances?

S: Well . . . when I gave friends a present, they always had to go out of the door, and then, if it was for example a picture of a pop star I would tear it a bit. So I was being nice to them, and the same time being evil because they didn't get anything too good.

Well, I have listened to many stories, but this was original. It was very honest of Susan to tell me about this sneaky behaviour which really is rooted in her self-worth as a child, her lack of love and her isolation. I talk about the child being condemned to live out themes represented by the parents:

A: It is not incorrect to call this inheritance a family curse which you will learn to eliminate in your life.

S: Family *curse*?

A: Yes. Something transferred from your mother connected with your self-esteem, and which you could fear you will transfer to your children . . . so that you might actually choose not to have children because of your own recollection of a childhood based on isolation and hurt pride.

S: Hm, I would like to have children – but it is true that I dare not have any at the moment . . . it isn't certain that I actually can have children . . .

A: That's right. There is actually a mechanism in you which can lead to spontaneous abortion . . . [the 5th house stellium]

S: Yes, I have had two miscarriages and one real abortion.

A: This is connected to a psychological state in which you do not permit anything to grow.

S: I haven't had a period for one and a half years, and nobody can understand why.

A: It's connected with your denial of the mother role. When you finally want to have a child you will have to overcome the saboteur within you.

S: Yes, but at times I want to be a mother . . . yet sometimes I don't think I will ever be. I have had a dream of having masses of children . . . maybe they won't be my own.

A: I also feel that you will have a lot to do with children, but it is more likely to be to a whole village of children in Africa or something [she had been talking about voluntary service overseas, which fitted well with her horoscope pattern] rather than an actual biological connection.

S: [Cheerfully] Well, perhaps it's a good thing that my husband has a child with another woman . . . then there *are* children [laughs].

The Saboteur

I feel that Susan's admission concerning giving gifts is significant. The past is interesting, but much more important is how past patterns are continued in the present. Awareness of past programming gives hope that the individual can have more control over personal fate. At this point we discuss other ways Susan can destroy present-day things. She would for example lie to her husband to revenge herself on him when she felt hurt – the badly aspected 7th house Mercury. This also explained how she reacted when he spoke to her about his dreams (reflecting her Sun–Neptune):

S: I wanted to show him that life wasn't necessarily beautiful and convince him that our love wasn't necessarily right or permanent.

A: So on the one hand you are sorry there is no love and security – and on the other you give the person

you love the impression that you don't believe in
the relationship . . . you make him unsure. Is that
right?

S: Hmm! Yes! I don't want people thinking that I'll be
there all the time.

A: What do you get out of that?

S: That I can pull out whenever it suits me . . . [Moon–
Uranus!] . . . I feel I have to convince him all the time
that I am a complete idiot. I have done the craziest
things just to show the worst sides of myself, so that
he will still say that he wants me.

So, she is still tearing up pictures. I know this manifestation of Pluto so well. Purging oneself. Wanting
others to accept the monster within. But it doesn't work,
there are no limits to Pluto's depths, and this way
leads only to exhaustion. I explain that she can live
without this psychic striptease. Later in life, when Pluto
is transformed from self-absorption to outer commitment
Susan's powerful 5th and 6th houses may show her
equipped to deal with suffering and transform the terrible
conditions other people suffer under. She can really help
people.

A: In healing others you will heal yourself. One advantage
you have is that no one can show you anything that will
shock you.

S: Yes, that's true.

A: You can work with people in real trouble, you don't
need to put down roots, you can live under difficult
conditions and move around. This suits you. You're the
gypsy type.

S: My mother actually comes from a gypsy family.

Oh!! Now I understand the Moon–Uranus–Pluto conjunction better . . . it's a real rootless inheritance! It's
about time the mother came into the picture.

Mum and Dad

The years 1965–1967 were of course classic years because of the rare Pluto–Uranus conjunction. The Moon personalises this area for Susan in some way, and this will obviously be related to some form of extreme experience of her mother. We try the direct approach:

A: If you didn't do what your mother wanted I suspect she totally ignored you – and made you feel you didn't exist. How did she do this?

S: I don't really know, but I remember some dreams that indicate this. Well, it was mostly that she got angry and I had to go to my room and shut up.

A: There were situations then when she just wouldn't talk to you? (Moon–Pluto square Mercury).

S: Yes, exactly. I was always frightened when I came home from school, and I had a guilty conscience. Maybe she was angry, maybe she was happy (Moon–Uranus). If she was in a bad mood I had to shut up and go to my room, but if she was in a good mood she would say [changes her voice to a high, weening tone], 'Come and have some tea and cake.' One never knew what she was mad about, but it was mostly my father who was [with feeling] a stupid pig . . . so her moods alternated like everybody else I guess.

A: So she wasn't mentally unbalanced?

S: Yes!

A: How?

S: She had breakdowns when she just cried and cried and cried.

A: So what did you do?

S: I cried with her, and screamed too. [The family curse, OK?]

A: With her?

S: [Resigned] With her.

A: Over?

S: Over my father. I have always hated my father – until a year ago when I talked to him, told him I loved him and that he was fine. I had only hated him because she hated him, I never knew why I hated him. Now I have virtually no communication with my mother.

A: So the scenario is that you were strongly emotionally manipulated by your mother [Moon conjunct Pluto–Uranus], but never had a clear picture of your father [Sun–Neptune intercepted in 6th].

S: My mother expected so much of me, everything I had to be . . . and I wasn't.

A: What should you be?

S: I had to be nice and proper, marry and get children.

A: [Laughs] Are you?

S: [Laughs] Not from her point of view. Of course I am in a terrible situation at the moment. She says it's my father's fault – all the awful things I have been through are my father's fault and she regrets . . .

A: [Interrupting] What did your father do?

S: Well, he was an alcoholic!

A: What for?

S: [Surprise] What for? Because of his failed life.

A: Failed?

S: Yes, considering his dreams and hopes about how things could have been . . . and weren't.

A: What wasn't he?

S: He was a butcher, but he wanted to be more than that . . . he would have liked to have been a vet [interesting Sun–Neptune in Scorpio 6th house theme here – butcher/vet: from destruction to healing!].

A: Did your mother tell you about his dreams?

S: No, nothing except that he was hopeless at everything, because he just drank and drank.

A: Do you remember someone else who drank and drank? [Her in Stockholm.]

S: Hmmm.

A: How do you think it feels to be despised by your wife?

S: Well, it's just terrible of course.

A: What can one do then?

S: [Giggles a little] Drink perhaps!

Now Susan is beginning to recognise and accept two archetypal areas in herself, the drinker and the hysteric, as a kind of emotional inheritance from her parents. Her parents are actually the vehicles of her karmic inheritance and as such have truly sacrificed themselves for her. Ultimately they cannot be blamed, and fortunately Susan's life is her responsibility. This means she can change it.

The T-Square

As ruler of her horoscope, Mercury's position at the apex of Susan's powerful T-square is crucial. It relates to her mother's scenes and imposed silence, but unfortunately it doesn't stop there as it will later affect communication in her adult relationships.

A: In stress situations, powerful arguments and exaggerated ultimatums tend to arise in your relationships. You put so much emotional energy into this that your partner may simply clam up [Mercury–Pluto] and not talk to you. Have you experienced this?

S: Yes! But I also experience the opposite, when I don't utter a word and become remote and almost untouchable. And also occasions when I become hellishly hysterical, shout and scream and throw things . . .

A: [Interrupts] Don't you get mad when you repeat your mother's patterns?

S: [Silence] Yes! But it takes a lot before I realise it's her. If I have to tell a child off I feel it's really like a curse when I hear her words coming out of my mouth. 'If you don't shut up I'll shout and wake the whole house,' she always used to say.

From here we go to the more positive sides of her T-square. How important it is to have a partner she can communicate and share ideas with, and how important it is to work in a position where there is a lot of activity and daily contact with a lot of people. Dealing with other people's feelings and resources on practical levels will be important [with Mars and Venus in in Capricorn in the 8th – a theme I go into later]. There may well be therapeutic and healing talents. The important thing is that Susan's dreams are converted to realities – unlike her father's. Obviously Pluto's transit over her Sun–Neptune conjunction in the mid-1990s will bring an important transformation here. A time to eliminate unrealistic dreams and get down to realities. This will be her big chance for self-realisation, but it is unlikely it will be achieved without therapy.

Yin and Yang

Whilst talking about interests and talents we of course get to the subject of health. With Sun–Neptune in the 6th house and the Moon in Virgo this is bound to be an important theme for her. She tells me of her interest in macrobiotics. I comment on a tendency to extremism in this area.

A: What happens when you visit your family?

S: I was home for Christmas for the first time in eight years – and I was a real monster. I was so provocative and had to poke around all the time in the most sensitive areas. They sat there and pigged themselves and sang – and of course there was nothing there I could eat, so I drank and was totally . . . yeah, I think I was evil and I managed in any case to ruin their Christmas, because I did not have the energy to go along with their hypocrisy and lies . . . they *had* to pretend to enjoy themselves . . . and then I went home and cried . . . and regretted my behaviour bitterly.

A: You eat macrobiotic food and try to live healthy, yet you drink a lot. How is this connected?

S: Well, I certainly don't feel that's a side of me . . . that ought to be there . . . it's just there at the moment . . . or it was there. Alcohol makes me more cold and there isn't anything that can hurt me any longer. I can choose to say, 'What the hell, now I'm going to drink.' Then I can handle the situation – then I don't have to sit and cry.

A: Over?

S: Over Christmas for example. All that. Then I don't get trapped . . . by their possessions, their opinions, their frustrations.

A: Does this area remind you of anything?

S: What do you mean? [Pause], My father?

A: Yes.

Of course as long as Susan rejects the spiritual ideals in herself as represented by her father, the dreamer, she will be condemned to see drinking as an aberration which has no connection with her true identity – which of course it does. By taking up contact with her father again she may be able to integrate this side of her nature in a healthy way. But back to the mother. Personal planets in Virgo aspecting Pluto often leads to exaggerated clearing-up compulsions, so:

A: What was your mother's attitude to tidying up?

S: Well she liked things to be neat and tidy. But we didn't have any money – everything was just old rubbish – but she liked it to be nice and in order.

A: She wasn't a fanatic then?

S: Yes!

A: She *was* a fanatic . . . OK.

S: She is still totally . . .

A: [Interrupting] Are you satisfied that you reflect these two sides of your parents? That you for example drink and smoke on the one hand and are an extreme vegetarian on the other?

S: [Laughs] No, I am not happy about it – at all!

By identifying strongly with one parent, Susan is forced to live out the other unconsciously. Extreme yin leads to yang and vice versa. Yet parents are good for something, it is just a question of being consciously selective. The ideal would be to integrate the intensity, discipline and survival power of the mother, with the vision and depth of the father.

We round off the consultation with a discussion of how she can consciously work with her positive inheritance and see through negative conditioning. This leads to a deeper discussion of Susan's present needs in relation to her husband, to whom she still feels a strong bond. Discussing the future possibilities as far as work is concerned, it dawns on Susan that she is not willing to return to the unhappy situation in Sweden with her husband at present. The chance she now has of working in an exotic country obviously exhilarates her and she leaves happy and hopeful about her prospects in this area. I have not forced this future scenario upon her – but it corresponds with the planetary patterns in her horoscope. Nobody can say that the future will be easy for Susan. Her chart shows many trials and challenges. But it also shows great strength and survival ability; and I am sure she would not have it any other way.

Themes in the Astrological Year

Working daily with consultations the astrologer truly has a finger on the astrological pulse of time – whether it is the monthly phase of the Moon or the thirty-year phase of Saturn. As the planets traverse the stellar landscapes their influences are modulated in subtle ways. But the keen eye of the astrologer learns to discern the transition phases as the planets change sign, and the variations of planetary expression as they aspect each other.

The outer planets provide a kind of backdrop to the hurried movements of the more personal planets – a backdrop which the astrologer gets used to and intimate with until suddenly an outer planet or group of outer planets changes sign. Astrologers quite clearly registered the profound change as both Pluto and Neptune moved out of Libra and Sagittarius and into Scorpio and Capricorn respectively. Fashions changed – labels and names were overtly displayed on the *outside* (Capricorn). Sexual habits changed as relationship experimentation (Pluto in Libra) gave way to greater emotional commitment – not unrelated to the threat of Aids (Pluto in Scorpio), and new ideals about morality (Neptune in Capricorn).

Similarly, with the monumental shift of the planetary forces of Uranus and Saturn from Sagittarius to Capricorn in 1988, the whole astrological framework was transformed. Pluto in Scorpio was no longer isolated but begins to receive support from the other heavyweights. A new emphasis on water and earth is felt – and heralded by the enormous earthquake in Armenia for example, political restructuring in the whole world. More curiously, it was at the time of the Saturn–Neptune conjunction in 1989 that scientists around the world struggled to create nuclear power with cold fusion – 'heavy water'. The religious revolution in Iran, and principles of economic *laissez-faire* in the West (Uranus in Sagittarius) makes way for drastic material changes of a more political nature in Russia and indeed the world. Expansion comes down to earth with a thud.

This change of scene heralds a completely different state of affairs in the consultation horoscope. Previously a client arriving with the Moon in the first degrees of Scorpio would be feeling under great emotional pressure and almost sure to encounter a radical and drastic upheaval reflected by the horary Moon's imminent conjunction with Pluto. But the 1989 scene shows Saturn sextiling Pluto – and although the client will still be in a difficult situation, this support from the outer planets will be reflected by a determination and resilience in the client. Instead of throwing the baby out with the bathwater, the client will be more inclined to launch a salvage operation. With three outer planets in Capricorn, everyone is trying harder. (On a political level this exact sextile was reflected in an international treaty limiting (Saturn) the production of plutonium!)

The astrological backdrop is important then and never quite repeats itself. There was a Uranus–Neptune–Saturn conjunction before – in 1306 – but that time it was in Scorpio. (This roughly coincided with the discovery and later use of gunpowder in the West.) Experiences with the consultation horoscope are most valid within their own framework of time, and can only be applied in a general form in future consultations. Nevertheless it might be instructive to have a look at one such period of time to see how both personal and political issues are reflected.

Mars and Venus – A Courting Ceremony

Anyone working with the consultation chart will soon discover that Venus and Mars will generally reflect the women and men talked about in the consultation. It helps in the consultation chart to allot roles to the planets in accordance with the client's personal story. If the client talks about a rich sister abroad and you see Venus in Taurus in the horary 9th, then you can safely identify Venus with the sister – and if Venus is about to make an opposition to Pluto you may also be able to predict a coming crisis in the sister's partnership situation. If a female client is concerned about the morality of her boss, and Mars is negatively aspected in Cancer (fall) in the 10th, you can safely allot this planet as significator for the boss, and if Mars is about to oppose Uranus, you may be able to predict a dramatic change in his situation. These planets may also represent other themes – for example Mars–Uranus may also reflect separation from the father early on in life, or a homosexual boss, and Venus–Pluto may reflect that taboo affair that the client had whilst on holiday – and this is all part of the fractal mandala of the horoscope.

As the planets closest to the Earth, Mars and Venus participate in a majestic waltz in their biennial conjunction cycle. During this period, Mars will move retrograde once and Venus perhaps twice, and this leads to a complicated interweaving of patterns which will actually be reflected in the love-lives of clients. The astrologer is privy to the human enactment of a divine drama reflected on every level of worldly life. The extraordinary cycle of Mars and Venus and its magical relation to the number 5 is well described in Alexander Ruperti's book *Cycles of Becoming*. Let us take a closer look at this cycle in the actual consultation.

We could take as our beginning point the so-called 'Harmonic Convergence' of August 1987, when all the 'traditional' planets formed a grand trine in fire signs. At this time the Sun, Moon, Mercury, Venus and Mars were in Leo, trine Saturn in Sagittarius and Jupiter in Aries. This emphasis on fire signs was supposed to coincide with a Galactic Initiation time prophesied many centuries previously in the Mayan calendar in what seems to be the Mayan equivalent to our Aquarian Age (José Arguelles, *The Mayan Factor*).

The actual conjunction between Mars and Venus took place at 1 degree Virgo. In the consultation this heralded a rather undramatic period in personal relationships – this was hardly the time for stormy romances or hidden affairs! One example typical of the period was the client whose problems centred around her secretarial duties in a Women's Lodge – the Rebecca Lodge (a delightfully Virgoan name). Naturally enough, she was left with all the work and it was affecting her health. Both Mars and Venus would later make a square to the Saturn–Uranus conjunction in Sagittarius – an indication that she would not put up with this for long.

Later Mars went into Libra – rather more interesting from the astrological point of view, because Mars is in detriment here. If we bear in mind the metaphor of the zodiacal signs as countries with the planets travelling through, we can see Mars far from home (Aries) in this sign and therefore forced to compromise to preserve integrity. Actually Mars in Libra in horary is a 'cad'. On occasion this represented the amorous man who perhaps had a string of relationships and couldn't be trusted, or was simply weak – especially because of Mars' square to Neptune in Capricorn.

As Venus was at this time in Scorpio and divested of all finery after her meeting with Pluto, it does not take much imagination to see what kind of situations arose. I remember one male client who had been married three times and still had a relationship with all three wives! At the same time many a female client came in crisis – Venus in Scorpio. Married women who after years of marriage had tasted the forbidden fruit of love with a younger and unreliable man (Mars in Libra square Neptune). There was fortunately a built-in escape mechanism for these people at this time however, because there was a mutual reception between Mars (which rules Scorpio) and Venus (which rules Libra). According to horary rules they can exchange places. Perhaps this means that Eve can replace the apple and return to the garden of Eden?

This period was also remarkable because of the Stock Market crash of October 1987. Here a Mercury stationary retrograde conjunction Pluto strengthened the negative effect of Venus in Scorpio. Wall Street shuddered over those few weeks, as Mercury went backwards and forwards over the early degrees of Scorpio. As Pluto's long transit of Scorpio will effect a transformation of the world economy and economic power blocks, upheavals can be expected every time there is a strong emphasis on this area from the personal planets. When Mars later moved into Scorpio, power issues really came to a head. This was a time when many big businessmen came for consultations – especially those involved in the computer industry. Pluto has a special connection with computers because of its influence on electronics and miniaturisation – the total transformation of society through control and information.

As one might expect, consultations at this time were characterised by heavy undercurrents and deep secrets. Hidden factors could easily be identified by studying the house in the horary chart that the Mars–Pluto conjunction occupied. Afternoon consultations in Scandinavia placed this conjunction in the 6th or 5th houses. Because of the high northerly latitude at which I work, Mars and Pluto were often intercepted – in other words the sign of Scorpio was contained within a larger house in the Placidus system. Intercepted houses tend to conceal the effect of the planets, and as Mars and Pluto are very secretive by nature of the taboo instinctive drives they can represent, it was very unlikely that a client would freely volunteer information. Yet secrets by their very nature absorb tremendous psychic energy and need to be shared or purged, so it often has a cathartic effect for the client to talk about them.

The Mars–Pluto in the 6th house often showed a very unpleasant situation in the working environment, with accompanying paranoia. A person might experience himself – rightly or wrongly – as victim of a smear campaign or vendetta. Sometimes there was a sexual aspect, for example being terrorised by the manager, or having a taboo affair with a colleague.

As Venus was in Capricorn during some of this period many professional women came into the consultation, and this led to some really complicated romantic involvements with powerful and ruthless men in the business world.

There were other variations of course as in the example given earlier of the male client with a secret desperate fear of Aids (see page 104).

With Pluto–Mars in the horary 5th I encountered even more dangerous possibilities, with themes of incest and really forbidden sexual contacts. One young woman was living with a considerably older man who had a 17-year-old son. This son was constantly making sexual overtures to her and she was torn between her 'stepmother' role and the physical attraction to a lad who was only a few years younger than herself. It is in the nature of Mars–Pluto contacts to be forced into a corner where a person is forced to be self-assertive. In this case the young woman decided to leave them both. A sensible decision.

One crucial issue of power during this Mars–Pluto conjunction was the fearful destructive power of the atomic bomb. At this time there was a milestone in American and Russian policies leading to modification of the MAD (Mutually Assured Destruction) doctrine. This outdated philosophy was really a manifestation of

Pluto in Libra (Balance of Power). It was in December 1987 that Gorbachev made his historic trip to America and signed a treaty leading to the destruction of destruction – Mars–Pluto – a mutual demolition of a proportion of the nuclear strike force. The horoscope for the signing is shown in Chart 5.3. As usual the astrological script-writers got it just right.

According to horary rules the host nation would be the 1st house – here represented by Aries and Mars. Gorbachev and Russia would be Libra and Venus – after all it was Gorbachev who travelled to a foreign country as the idealist and peacemaker – Venus conjunct Neptune in the 9th. And quite clearly he succeeded in containing the destructive power of the American military colossus symbolised by Mars–Pluto. It is interesting to see how during the four minutes it took to sign the necessary documents Mars and Pluto became intercepted in the 7th house. It is by the way a striking astrological fact

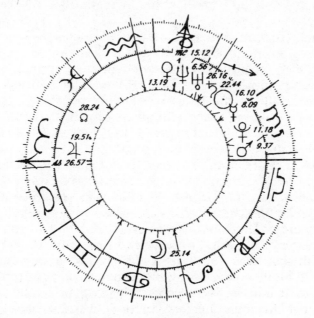

Chart 5.3: 8 Dec. 1987, 19.06 GMT Washington

that some of the greatest diplomatic breakthroughs occur with Sun–Saturn conjunctions.

After the fascinating sojourn of Mars in Scorpio, it entered Sagittarius whilst Venus was for the most part in Pisces. A completely different flavour. Venus is said to be exalted in Pisces – but this does not necessarily mean a happy love-life! It just means that the finest qualities of the soul are exhibited.

I remember that a TV series was running at this time set in eighteenth-century France. In the main female role was a very religious woman who slaved away for her many children. The man was restless and desperate for adventure, so he informed his wife that he was going to emigrate alone to Canada. Did she shout at him? Did she stab him to death? No; true to the spirit of Venus in Pisces she took on her cross of suffering and prayed for him while he slept! He later regretted leaving her and sailed back from Canada but unfortunately drowned. Well, Mars conjuncted Saturn and Uranus in Sagittarius. Justice was done!

In the consultation this situation reflected itself in similar themes. Women seemed content with the dream of love, even if the reality was different. The man abroad, or the foreign man was often a factor (Mars in Sagittarius). One woman told of the letters containing poetry which she received from a Japanese admirer – in strong contrast to the strong sexuality of Mars in Scorpio it was the higher ideals that became accentuated here.

When Mars later moved into Capricorn, its sign of exaltation, the horary astrologer might have expected finer manifestations of this planet's influences. Yet Mars had to meet Neptune here and this resulted in a dissipation of its energy. The most classic example I had of this was the male client who came with an exact Mars–Neptune conjunction in the 5th house. Here was a happily married man who wanted nothing more than to add to his brood of two daughters. The theme of children and family comes up here through the Leo Ascendant and Moon–Venus opposition on the MC–IC axis. Unfortunately no matter how hard he tried he could not seem to make his wife pregnant. Yet in the consultation chart the dominant Moon–Venus opposition (which also existed in the natal chart) here on the Taurus–Scorpio axis could suggest a tendency to indulge in taboo pleasure-orientated activities, amongst other things. Mars–Neptune's associations with drugs suggested that this might be a factor in preventing fertilisation. He confirmed that he did smoke marijuana. Although he felt there was nothing wrong with his potency, the horoscope suggests that the spermatazoa were at least confused! *Their* goal was obviously unclear – Mars–Neptune in the 5th. I suggested to him that he gave up the drug, at least for a period, which he did. Happily his wife became pregnant within two months – actually indicated by the passage of the MC–IC axis over the Moon–Venus opposition.

Once Mars extracted himself from Neptune's clammy embrace, the tales of alcoholics and drug-misusers ebbed off, and the exaltation of Mars seemed to take effect. Men were ambitious, serious and responsible – though Capricorn tended to undermine self-confidence – and with Venus entering Taurus, the typical woman in the consultation was stable and had dignity. This was really a fine period in the spring of 1988 with the hard-working man and the stable family. Even when Venus in Taurus confronted Pluto by opposition, she seemed to retain her strength and dignity – something I have also found to be the case with the Moon opposing Pluto from Taurus where it is exalted. A planet in its own sign or exaltation simply has the resources to handle adversity with dignity.

With Mars' entry into Aquarius a period of extremism began. Mars in Aquarius really does tend to be an outsider – the odd-man-out at a party. As Aquarius has political and social overtones, this was most noticeable on the national arena. Thus in France the extreme right-wing leader Le Penn had sweeping success in elections, just as in Denmark the extreme right secured more seats in the parliament giving them a controlling position. In the consultation, men represented by Mars in Aquarius were stubborn and independent, and very unwilling to be tied down.

It was at this time that Venus went into Gemini, where she was to spend the next four months because of retrograde movement. This was an extraordinary journey for Venus and a fine illustration of sign borders and retrograde movement. Venus actually made an entry into Cancer and went retrograde at 0°27' precisely opposite Uranus at 0°10' Capricorn. It is as if they joined arms and returned together into the mutable experience of Gemini–Sagittarius (see Figure 5.1).

Anyone with personal planets at zero degrees cardinal signs is bound to recall extreme experiences at this time. If we look at the graph we can see that while Venus dithers in Cancer from the 18th to the 27th May 1988, Mercury moves into position at 26 degrees Cancer waiting to receive the wounded maiden with open arms. Mercury does after all rule Gemini, and is only too happy to entertain the lady of love for as long as possible. Mercury then leads Venus back to 18 degrees Gemini where they slowly part company again as Mercury moves direct and leaves a still retrograde Venus.

What does this planetary tango mean in human terms? One unifying factor in many consultations with the retrograde Venus was the confirmed single woman. She might have affairs and uncommitted relationships (Gemini), but she was most interested in her friendships and children. The encounter with Uranus and the short sojourn in Cancer often represented a past flirtation with family life, only to have her fingers burned. Many female clients told of painful divorces in the past which had convinced them that it was far better to go it alone, develop themselves intellectually (Mercury–Venus) and concentrate on mental, rather than emotional satisfaction. This was the time of the skilled and independent professional woman.

In political life there were actually a number of scandals concerning women. Issues that came up and were dropped when Venus was direct were taken up again when Venus

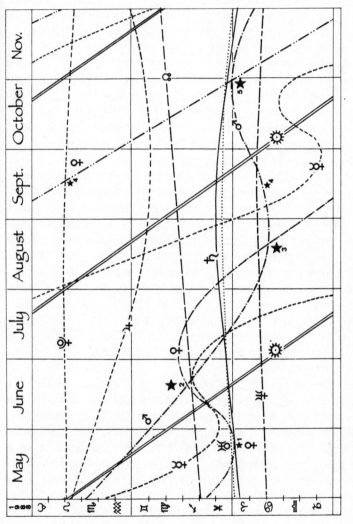

Fig. 5.1 Planetary Movements May–Nov. 1988

hit Uranus and went retrograde. Both the Swedish Minister for Justice (a woman) lost her job because of attempts to gather secret intelligence, and the Danish Minister for Health was accused of lying and nearly lost her job.

It is interesting to note that as Venus moved into 0 degrees Cancer, Mars simultaneously moved into 0 degrees Pisces. This trine between water signs was full of promises, but the goods were certainly not delivered. Water sign trines are rather suspect in horary because they are based on emotional issues but do not necessarily bring concrete results. When Mars trined Venus here he caught Venus at a turning-point, shocked and vulnerable opposing Uranus from Cancer. As Mars proceeded through his dreamy Piscean world, Venus had already reneged on all promises and run into the arms of Mercury – fickle lady. The female client's experience of men at this time was as unrealistic and unreliable (Mars in Pisces), but the man's experience of the woman was one of confusion at her apparent about-face. Many a male client at this time proceeded with his family plans, long after the woman had made her declaration of independence. But when Venus went back from her premature trine to Mars to meet him by square (from Gemini to Pisces), the acute mental differences between male and female became more apparent.

Finally, in July 1988, Mars came home to Aries, reborn and rejuvenated with boyish enthusiasm and naïvety. Let us not forget that the period from July to November 1988 saw the closing stages of the election campaign between Bush and Dukakis. Was Bush a *man* or was he a mouse? Not wishing to leave the electorate in doubt, both contendants played the role of 'real men' (Mars in Aries), with Dukakis being filmed driving a tank, should anyone be in doubt about *his* manhood. This was an extraordinary period because Mars went retrograde at 11 degrees Aries and was to spend six months in the sign Aries before rushing into decadence in Taurus. But the months leading up to the American election were dominated by the Mars–Neptune square and the station of Mars at 29°53' Pisces a week prior to the election.

Mars' station in Pisces took place in the square to Saturn and Uranus. Those who followed the election may remember the furore concerning the advertising tactics (Pisces) of the Bush campaign. One particularly successful ploy was the juxtaposition in a TV advertising campaign of blacks being let out of gaol with the terrorisation and rape of white women, appealing to the lowest racist impulses of the electorate. This was a reference to the case of Willie Horton, a black released on parole in Dukakis' own state, who later committed murder. The sign Pisces often relates to the black population (slavery) and of course Pisces relates to prisons, and Mars square Saturn–Uranus to violence.

The Democrats were, however, not slow to make capital out of the scandal concerning the coming Vice-President Quayle. It turned out that he had used his influence to avoid being sent to Vietnam in the early seventies – Mars–Neptune again: definitely not a real man there!

When all was said and done, Bush and Dukakis were men of their time, one with a natal Mars–Neptune opposition and the other with a natal square, but Bush was more successful at conducting an advertising smear campaign. The turning-point of Mars at the beginning of November also heralded a turning-point for the Democratic campaign after months of setbacks. Indeed it seemed that Mars reflected the fortunes of Dukakis, perhaps because he is a Scorpio. While it was direct he appeared to be winning hands down over Bush. But when it went retrograde his fortunes turned and Dukakis went on the defensive. In the closing stages Venus entered her own sign Libra in direct opposition to Mars, who was still weakened by his deathly station at 29 degrees Pisces (conjunct the unfortunate star Scheat). The Democratic wagon had no time to gain speed and the election went to the Venusian Bush.

While there was a drama being played out on the world stage, minor dramas were happening in the consultation. I have many examples of consultations from the period when Mars was stationary in the last degree of Pisces. One woman rang up having met the love of her life at a disco, but she had no address or telephone number where she could contact him afterwards (Venus in Virgo opposition Mars, square Saturn–Uranus). Would she see him again? (No!) Another client had planned to give up her job to sail across the Atlantic with her boyfriend (Mars in Pisces). He left suddenly without her but accompanied by another maiden.

The example in Chart 5.4 is of a film director (Mars rules the Ascendant in Pisces) who telephoned from abroad. This man was very unhappy. All he wanted to do was sit at home and drink himself into oblivion (Mars in Pisces in the 4th). His wife was having an affair with a younger American (note Moon in Gemini conjunct retrograde Jupiter in the 7th). She had run up an enormous phone-bill ringing him in America (Moon–Jupiter in Gemini – Jupiter, retrograde and in detriment has no dignity here).

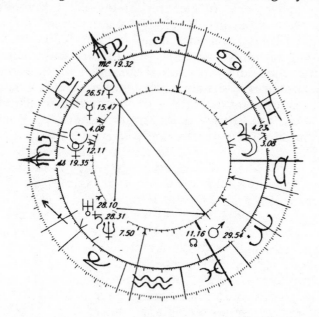

Chart 5.4: 27 Oct. 1988, 8.15 GMT Oslo

Venus is also the significator of the wife and is extremely badly placed in fall and square Saturn–Uranus.

Obviously both of them are feeling weak and insecure, but Mars here is at its weakest, a fact profoundly testified to by my client who was drowning his sorrows at home and had given up the film he was supposed to be directing.

It is truly a privilege to be witness to the amazing correlation of events varying from small private happenings to world dramas. The astrologer working with horary tunes in to the moment, and as a result his life reflects the moment. Clients become part of a greater story, welded through the consciousness of the astrologer into a universal unfoldment of cosmic principles in the endless cycle of the planets.

The astrologer is both actor and observer in the cosmic dance and as such has the ability to transcend the imprisoning cycle of time through observing his own actions and words – and the client's. Client and astrologer are interwoven into one plane of existence and the client comes to live out a considerable amount of the astrologer's personal karma. The astrological counsellor will discover that his personal transits are represented through the life and experience of the client, and this of course means that the consultation process is a kind of symbiotic process of mutual help. It is the client's fate to meet the astrologer – and vice versa. This is their mutual good fortune.

6

New Times

And I saw a new heaven and a new earth . . .

Revelation ch. 21 V.1

The Mutable Crucifixion

It is probable that people living in any period of history feel that they live in a world of change and transition to a greater or lesser extent. But humans living in the twentieth century are in a special dilemma. Technological change has raced ahead at such a speed that the individual today is left gasping for breath still grasping the past. In the last few hundred years the population has increased exponentially and is apparently threatening to swamp Earth's resources. In the year 1700 there were about 7½ million people in Britain; now there are 60 million. There were only a few million people in Northern America; now there are a quarter of a billion. At the same time strict religious moral codes have broken down and an era of permissiveness sweeps aside restrictive philosophies of the past. Moral lapses treated as major heresies only a few hundred years ago now scarcely raise an eyebrow. Pollution experts proclaim the Earth is sick. Industrial growth consumes world resources as if it were a malicious disease, and the human parallels – cancer, heart and lung diseases proclaim that the human being is sick. What is going on?

The tremendous increase in population and seething activity on Earth has an interesting parallel in the human body. There comes a stage in pregnancy when the exponential growth of foetus cells ceases as the major organs, brain and body of the coming child become fully formed. After the third month of pregnancy this rapid growth process ends and more stable conditions ensue. For the mother this sudden invasion of her body by a foreign entity can be a very disturbing process leading to vomiting and general discomfort.

The Earth is pregnant, and amidst the groans and cries of a teeming population, a new birth is imminent. Pisces is making way for Aquarius – and Pisces is the mother of Aquarius. There is much talk about the Age of Aquarius, but those of us incarnate today exist very much with the consciousness of Pisces, and the transition experience to Aquarius is accompanied by discomfort, sickness and pain. The birth is slow and laboured and cannot take place within a single lifespan – it is gradual process spanning many generations.

The calendar in the Western world is based on the birth of Jesus Christ – an extraordinary testimony to the avatar of the Piscean age, who sacrificed himself for our sins and suffered on the cross for the salvation of humanity. History is divided into BC (before Christ) and AD (Anno Domini – the year of the Master). His cross – and ours – is the mutable cross of Pisces – Virgo and Gemini–Sagittarius, and the crucifixion of Christ can be seen as the incarnation of the Piscean principle in matter. The word Christ derives from the Greek *Xythios*, which means fish, and the symbolism of the fish can still be seen in various church apparel, the bishop's mitre and other church accoutrements. The New Testament is full of symbolism concerning the Virgo–Pisces polarity telling for example of the feeding of the multitudes with five loaves and two fishes, and the anointing of Jesus's feet (Pisces) by Martha. In St John we can read how Christ as an example to his disciples washed their feet saying that to clean the feet was eqivalent to cleansing the body totally (John 13:10). This humble act was an example of the spirit of humility and service (Pisces – Virgo) which were the key virtues of the Age. With the later spreading of the Christian message throughout the Roman Empire, and the subsequent persecution of its practitioners, Christians actually identified themselves to each other by tracing the form of a fish with their hands.

Basic Catholic worship is centred on the Virgin Mary and Christ on the cross. Jesus tells Simon and Peter 'I will make you fishers of men' and in Matthew 11:34 we can read:

> Think not that I am come to bring peace on earth: I came not to send peace, but a sword. For I am come to set a man at variance against his father, and the daughter against her mother.

The mutable cross is an extreme polarity and the Christian age manifested this polarity and brought suffering. Christ brought the sword to create polarity. This was the polarity of God and Mammon, Catholicism and Protestantism, Communism and Capitalism, light and dark, God and Devil, good and evil, spirit and matter. Issues in the Christian era are seen as black and white leading to one of two alternatives – heaven or hell. Twentieth-century philosophers preach another reality however. French existentialists after the war subscribed to the view that 'Hell is within us,' and psychologists work at liberating and befriending the energy tied up in complexes – the devils within.

The Age of Pisces saw the introduction of baptism by water, and the holy men of the age were those who martyred themselves for their faith. Faith was an essential quality of this last age; Knowing will be the essential quality of the next. The spirit of suffering and sacrifice (Pisces) brought out the finest qualities in man, and the highest followers of the Christian religion retired to monasteries and nunneries to commune privately with their Lord – a recognisable Piscean characteristic. Christ's exhortation was: 'He that loseth his life for my sake shall find it.' When asked by Peter what his followers would gain Jesus responded: 'Ye which have followed me, in the regeneration when the Son of Man shall sit in the throne of glory, ye also shall sit on the twelve thrones, judging the twelve tribes of Israel.'

There are many references to the twelve tribes of Israel in the Bible and there seems to be good reason to see them as a reference to the twelve zodiacal signs (see for example Genesis 49). Jesus saw himself as a man called upon by God to act out the cosmic sacrifice as symbolised by Pisces. His actions and events in his life still shape the experience of our year, our national holidays and indeed spending habits (Christmas). But more than that his spirit, and the spirit of suffering is incarnate in every one of us born in the 2,000 years since his birth. This literal incarnation of Christ into matter, as expressed through his words ('This is my body, This is my blood') at the Last Supper is still celebrated in the ritual of the Eucharist – the ceremonial partaking of bread (Virgo) and wine (Pisces). It is important to understand that Christ literally incarnated into matter as the Piscean Age dawned, to be able to grasp the transformation from one age to another which is taking place now. Christ was clearly aware of the coming age and often referred to the 'Age of Man' – Aquarius.

For us born under the galactic influences of Pisces it might seem unthinkable that the spirit of the Piscean Age and the experience of guilt and suffering will ever disappear, but Aquarian consciousness is something quite different, and free of the polarities and strife of the previous age. Suffering and guilt are not major factors in the Aquarian Age, neither is the spirit of withdrawal and retirement. There will be no one figure worshipped in this age and no élite (as in the priesthood). Aquarius is the Age of Man and the property of every man and woman. When people look back 2,500 years from now at the beginnings of the new age, they will see the figures of American presidents carved out of the mountains (Mount Rushworth) and understand that the Aquarian Age was the age of freedom, brotherhood and equality – the principles of the French Revolution.

The Human Arrow

The transition from one age to another, as the polar axis makes its slow 26,000 year wobble through the twelve signs, is not just a galactic phenomenon. It is not as if the New Age takes us unawares as we look on passively, for we are ourselves the agents of this change, albeit unconsciously. The purpose of the Piscean Age was to engineer Aquarius. At our stage of development on Earth today we are the quintessence of the universe, star stuff. We are not just accidents in space, but rather the natural consequence of the unfoldment of the universe since the big bang ten thousand million years ago. After the first generation of stars created the more complex elements like carbon and oxygen from the *prima materia* of hydrogen and helium, and then exploded as supernovas, our own solar system and planets were formed – about five thousand million years ago. We now find ourselves in a position to study and understand the universe because it takes exactly this long for intelligent life to evolve and explore its home. In the expanding universe evolved human life can only manifest at this exact time – at least in this area of this universe.

This concept of the human situation is actually en-shrined in a scientific principle called the 'anthropic principle'. In answer to the question 'Why is the universe the way we see it?', the anthropic principle says simply: 'If it had been different, we would not be here!' (See Stephen Hawkins, *A Brief History of Time*, Bantam Press.)

Humans find themselves at the tip of the arrowhead of time, co-authors of their fate. As we learn to master the material of which we are made – the world of matter – we experience a corresponding expansion of awareness and of our spatial boundaries. That is why the technological changes around us at the moment are crucial to our development. It is true that we humans create havoc in the world around us and leave deep wounds in Mother Earth, but the polluted body of the earth will heal because the very momentum of technological development will be enough to carry us into a new, clean age based on a 'clean' low-energy technology. It is the transition, the pregnancy, which wounds the body.

As human consciousness moves from the feet (and the wheel), to the ankles (taking flight), there is a whole new play of elements, with air of course dominating. Air pollution is basically the result of old technologies in the transition period – a consequence of the burning of organic materials. It is the primitive use of the element of fire, which harms the atmosphere on the one hand, and depletes Earth's resources on the other. Hitler was a great believer in the power of the fire element, and actually visualised his war against Russia as the conquering of ice by fire. We know different, however, because it was ice that was the victor in that battle! And indeed ice – supercooling, 'cool' technologies, electronics – and the principle of Scorpio as part of the fixed Aquarian Cross, will be a dominating factor in the New Age.

The Aquarian Age is a 'cool' age, and there will be very little use of the element of fire. This will be a major characteristic of the age – very little burning. Heat will be won more directly from energy waves, and low-energy electronic technology will drastically reduce the need for huge centralised energy production. Fire is anathema to Aquarius and will have no place in that electronic and plastic environment. Radiation and wave forms will be the energy form on which the Age is founded. It will simply be a radioactive Age – pollution will be in the more subtle form of all forms of microwaves and radiation which penetrate our bodies. Whilst this can seem life-threatening and in some cases will be, it is worth remembering what life was like in Europe in the last age. The majority of people worked from morning to night with no let-up, because otherwise they would not survive. They died young, if not as a result of war or disease, then simply from being worn out. The average life-span was between 40 and 50. Infant mortality was high. People really suffered.

Aquarian Dawn

Astrologers have often concerned themselves with setting a date for the beginning of the Age of Aquarius, and I would like to take a look at two important charts later. But those who have eyes to see will see Aquarius around us *now* – not in some technical or intellectual way, but in the very fabric of our lives at this very time. In actuality there is no sharp dividing line, simply because the constellations have no sharp borders, and flow gently into each other. Some constellations are enormous – for example Pisces, and some, like Aquarius, take up much less space. In Hindu astrology, which is based on the constellations or sidereal zodiac, they do, however, have quite definite borders for the beginning of each star sign, based on particular prominent stars. Western astrology is based on the tropical zodiac which sets the first point of Aries at the Spring Equinox when the Sun crosses the equator and day and night are equal in length. As such our astrology is not actually based on 'star' signs but on a twelvefold division of the Earth's path around the Sun.

Because of an irregularity in the rotation of the Earth on its polar axis in relation to the plane of the Ecliptic, the Spring equinoctial point is seen to move backwards in relation to the fixed stars, rather as a spinning top describes a circle when it wobbles (see Figure 6.1). The yearly movement is almost imperceptible – about 50' per year, but after seventy-two years the equinoctial point moves backwards a whole degree in relation to the zodiac.

After 25,870 years the polar axis has made a majestic sweep through all twelve signs, and this period of time is called a Great Year, or Platonic Year. This means that an astrological age lasts 2,155 years as the polar axis sweeps through one sign of the zodiac. Theoretically, then, many years have yet to elapse before the new age, if we were to date the beginning of the last age at AD 1. In actual fact, according to some schools of Hindu astrology the correspondence between the sidereal and tropical zodiacs took place in the third century AD, which would mean that the new age would approximately begin around the year 2400. The difference between the two zodiacs is calculated at present to be 23½ degrees. This difference is called the *Ayanamsa* and has to be subtracted from the ephemeris positions of the planets to convert them to Hindu positions. Accordingly it would take another four centuries for the equinoctial point to leave Pisces and enter the last degree of Aquarius.

It is possible that the astronomical beginning of the Aquarian Age *is* at this time – a few hundred years is little in historical perspective – but I doubt it. To imagine another 400 years elapsing is to deny the evidence of our

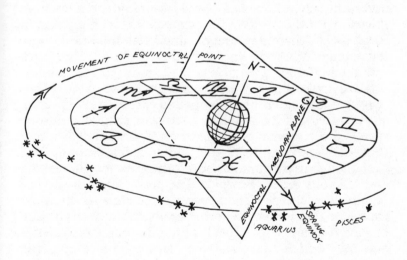

Figure 6.1: Precession

own eyes, because the dawn of Aquarius is here now affecting every fibre of our bodies, as I will attempt to show over the next pages.

A major factor in the timing of the Aquarian Age, and in traditional mundane astrology generally, is the twenty-year conjunction cycle of Saturn and Jupiter. This cycle has always been used by astrologers as a measure of trends and changes in the evolution of history. The fascinating thing about this conjunction cycle is that it takes place in one particular element for a period of approximately 200 years, and then moves on to the next element – fire, earth, air, water; fire, earth, air, water, etc. The change from one element to another is called 'The Great Mutation' and is seen to represent vast collective shifts in the affairs of men.

The shift from one element to another is not exactly regular, and if we refer to the table we can see that a new mutation is always heralded by a 'maverick' sign before the new series of Saturn–Jupiter conjunctions in a new element. For example in 1604 and 1624, when there was a conjunction in Sagittarius and Leo before the last water conjunction in Pisces in 1644. There was also a maverick conjunction in Virgo in 1802 heralding the coming Earth mutation phase for example. And in 1980 there was a maverick conjunction in Libra heralding the coming air mutation.

If we look at the water mutation between 1424 and 1644 we can identify this period as a very spiritual and introverted time when a deeply religious Europe searched a conscience divided between Catholicism and Protestantism because of the Lutheran reformation. The Catholic Church counterattacked through the Inquisition and religious terror (Scorpio). The persecution of witches became widespread. Other events characterising the water trinity in this period were for example the introduction of slavery (Pisces) as a result of the discovery of America and the need for labour there. The habit-forming drug tobacco started to enslave Europe (it was considered so dangerous in seventeenth-century France that it was only

YEAR	♃ ♄	YEAR	♃ ♄	♅	♆	♇
(AIR)		EARTH				
1384	♊	1842	♑			
1404	♒	1861	♍			
WATER		1881	♉			
1424	♏	1901	♑			
1444	♋	1921	♍	♒		
1464	♓	1940	♉			
1484	♏	1961	♑			
1504	♋	1981	♎			
1524	♓	2000	♉	♒	♒	
1544	♏	AIR				
1564	♋	2020	♒			♒
1584	♓	2040	♎			
1603	♐ ♌	2060	♊			
1623	♌	2080	♒ ♊	♒		
1643	♓	2100	♎			
FIRE		2120	♊			
1663	♐	2140	♒			
1684	♌ ♈	2160	♏	♒	♒	
1704	♈	2179	♊			
1723	♐ ♌	2199	♒			
1742	♌ ♈	WATER				
1762	♈	2219	♏			
1782	♐	2239	♋ ♒			
1802	♍ ♈	2259	♓			
1822						

Figure 6.2: Saturn/Jupiter conjunction cycle as catalyst for the New Age

available on prescription!). And towards the end of this period Europe was decimated by the plague. On a much brighter note was the introduction of tea – absolutely the best thing to come out of this period! Wars in this period were characterised by religious convictions.

With the coming of the great mutation in fire from 1663 to 1822 a new spirit of rationality was developed, devoid of the blind emotionalism of the water trinity. This was the great period for philosophers like Rousseau, who saw man in union with nature, and Descartes, who was concerned with the relation between mind and matter. Newton's theories of energy were developed and were to dominate scientific thinking up to the present age. The eighteenth century witnessed a veritable explosion of revolutionary passion which rocked civilisation. The urge to travel and explore the newly acquired colonies led to a tremendous pioneering spirit in Europe leading to colonisation of every conceivable corner of the Earth. The boundaries of space opened up through the telescope and frontiers expanded in every direction. Wars in this period were characterised by conflicts of interest over expansion.

After the scientific fervour of the fire mutation a new cycle of conjunctions began in earth in 1842 heralding the systematic exploitation of the Earth's resources made possible by the previous subjection of the Third World. This was really the beginning of the Age of Materialism and consumer consciousness, reflected in a myriad of political and economic theories – not least the dialectical materialism of Communism. The race was now on to grab as much as possible of what was going in the different colonies around the world. Huge machines were developed to gouge precious raw materials out of the ground (Taurus) to make a vast range of products (Virgo). These products went through various stages of refinement until they ended up in a proliferation of shops and stores (Capricorn) to satisfy the demands of the customer. That's us. To get a good idea of the effect of this earth mutation, go into your local supermarket! At the same time scientific development has pierced deeper and deeper into the nature of matter itself, culminating in the realisation that matter is another expression of energy. This awareness has not truly seeped into collective consciousness yet – for it is a property of the air trinity soon to dawn. Wars during the period of the earth mutation have been characterised by the desire for land and the greed for resources.

And this is where we stand now – definitely on the verge of a new mutation – into *air*. And not before time, because the Earth itself has been raped of its air, its minerals, its water and its trees. But this state of affairs cannot last because our consciousness has moved on and we have learned what we had to learn during the earth mutation. Over the next forty years materialistic principles will evaporate and the attention of human consciousness will be focused in completely new areas. The maverick conjunction in Libra in 1980 has already announced the air mutation's coming, and after a last earth conjunction in Taurus in the year 2000 a new spirit dawns upon the Earth. We already have a foretaste of what this is as a result of the transformation of communication afforded by satellites and computer technology. But the mental network between individuals and nations is just a shadow of what is in store for us when the air mutation takes over.

Transition

There is no shortage of charts put forward by astrologers for the Aquarian Age! These vary from the eighteenth century to well into the next millennium. They are either based on varying Hindu ayanamsas, or personal astrological preferences (particularly the theosophical hopes concerning Krishnamurti, who was groomed to be avatar of the New Age – and wisely refused the 'privilege'), on the writings of seers like Nostradamus and on other considerations. In presenting the air mutation chart for the year 2020, I do not wish to add to the confusion. There are many turning-points, and many moments of transition in the long historic process. Many of the horoscopes drawn will capture the essence of the age – though some will capture the folly of the astrologer!

Yet the air mutation chart will be a basic chart for the Aquarian transition, certainly being as relevant for the next two centuries as the earth mutation chart was for the last two centuries. This chart is based on the exact conjunction of Jupiter and Saturn at half a degree Aquarius – the first conjunction in Aquarius since 1404. The Great Air Mutation actually begins in the Aquarius air sign inaugurating a 200-year period of air sign influence. I have set the chart for New York because Uranus, the planet of the New Age, rises in New York at this time, and because America is the cradle of the next age, and New York the melting-pot of the old age culture.

There is an important mundane tradition for calculating the Great Mutation chart, and this has been well researched by Charles Harvey for exampie in the classic *Mundane Astrology* (Aquarian Press). Chart 6.1 is the chart for the great mutation in earth which took place on 26 January 1842. Chart 6.2 is the air mutation of 2020. Of course these charts can be calculated for any world capital, but by choosing Berlin in the first chart, it is possible to see how the great upheavals on the European stage in the nineteenth and twentieth centuries key in to this basic chart.

Charles Harvey has documented how the foundation of the German Empire took place as planets touched off key points in this chart, and how Hitler's chart likewise activated both charts through an astonishing array of midpoint contacts (*Mundane Astrology*, page 394). Thus Hitler's Moon–Jupiter conjunction fell precisely on the mutation Ascendant and Saturn–Jupiter conjunction, his Uranus opposition mutation Pluto, his IC on mutation Sun – to mention only a few contacts. Because of the unique connections between Germany's horoscope and the earth mutation chart, Germany and Hitler became a natural 'earth' for this era.

Just as the earth mutation chart was of major significance

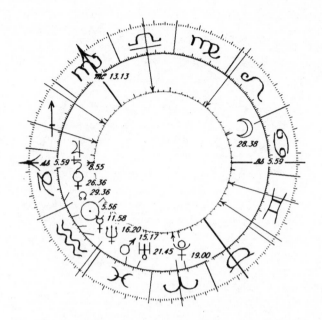

Chart 6.1: 26 Jan. 1842, 5.29 GMT Berlin

for the last 200 years, the air mutation chart for 2020 will be an effective chart for the twenty-first and twenty-second centuries – and possibly for the whole Aquarian Age, with New York the most dramatic point of change. Piscean principles will still be dominant, and in a harmonious manner, because Neptune is in Pisces at this time, and its energies are distributed by its conjunction with the Moon. There will still be those who choose isolation as an alternative to enforced socialisation. In the earth mutation chart of 1842 Aquarian energies were dominant through the inventiveness symbolised by Neptune in Aquarius, conjunct Mercury and the Sun.

A rather disconcerting element about the air chart is the exact square between Mars in Aries and Pluto in Capricorn. There could be a certain amount of destructiveness concerned with the demolition of old systems of business and administration (Pluto in Capricorn). I must

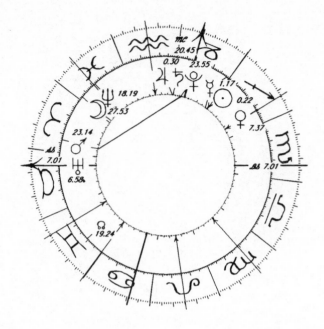

Chart 6.2: The Aquarian Mutation: 21 Dec. 2020, 18.18 GMT, New York

say, there is a rather totalitarian quality about this Mars–Pluto square which could suggest secret government enforcement processes harmonising with some of the more negative political aspects of Aquarius. This Mars–Pluto square activates the Mars–Saturn conjunction of the United Nations horoscope (Chart 6.3) exactly. Other contacts to this chart suggest that the United Nations may have considerable power in some form of world government in the future.

The chief function of this air trinity is to disseminate and spread knowledge and to effect a social integration of world populations. It is interesting to see that the Saturn–Jupiter conjunction falls almost exactly on the North Node of the earth mutation chart, and as such shows the fulfilment of the solar purpose as indicated

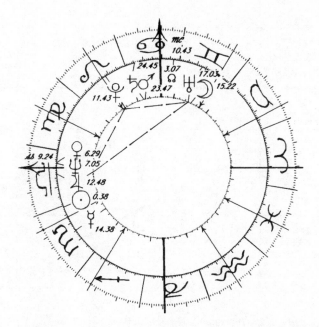

Chart 6.3: United Nations, 24 Oct. 1945, 4.45 EST, Washington DC

by the 1842 Node. In the air chart the North Node falls in Gemini, which is a general indication of the whole tone of communication, curiosity and openness which characterises the coming era. This node contacts exactly the Uranus–Moon conjunction of the New-York-based United Nations, which is a symbol of the smelting together of world peoples through communication. Wars in the air mutation period – in so far as they are possible in a global society – will be based on control of the airwaves, and influence on the minds of populations.

In itself the beginning of the air mutation at zero Aquarius just after the beginning of a new millennium is adequately strong symbolism to justify this time as the beginning of the Age of Aquarius. But there are many other purely astrological factors which show the total domination of the Aquarian influence as we move into the twenty-first century. When we consider the profound

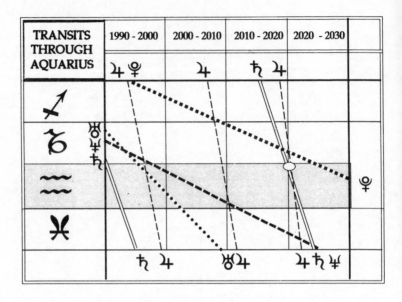

Fig. 6.3 Planetary movements 1990–2020

effect of Uranus when it move into Sagittarius, or of Neptune when it moved into Capricorn, or Pluto when it moved into Scorpio, we cannot help but be impressed by the planetary line-up at the beginning of the next century (see Figure 6.3).

Both Uranus and Neptune are in Aquarius in the year 2000, and Pluto later moves into this sign some time after the Great Mutation takes place. Even if we had no physical evidence as to the transition to a new age, this is an impressive astronomical testimonial to the powerful new influence of Aquarius. Just as clearly we must accept that our experience of the Aquarian influence in the last years of the twentieth century – powerful as this is – is nothing compared with what is to come.

Rumblings

Despite the astrological promise of the future, there is a period in our lifetimes which we cannot ignore as a significant moment for the dawning of the New Age. For those of us who lived through the idyllic years of faith and innocence in the sixties, there can be no doubt that a taste of Aquarius was experienced. This was the time of 'Flower Power' – a fitting description of the influence of Pluto in Virgo in this decade. Youth and Age were polarised in the mid-sixties – when Saturn in Pisces opposed Uranus (and Pluto) in Virgo; and young people sought consciousness transformation through drug-induced euphoria – Neptune in Scorpio. Looking back at this period there is a natural tendency to distance oneself from the naïvety of the time, and feel almost embarrassed at the words that were in the mouths of many influential cultural figures – Love and Peace. With the dawn of the seventies times had changed and this change was encapsulated in the memorable words of John Lennon: 'The dream is over; now we have to get back to so-called reality.'

It was in the sixties that man expanded into space, with Russian and American space teams competing to be first on the Moon. The Americans succeeded first of course – at the time of the exact conjunction of Jupiter and Uranus in 1969. Down on Earth, young people were turning on, tuning in – and dropping out. They no longer wanted to be a part of the reality machine sold to them by the post-War adult generation. In the forefront of this consciousness revolution were musical figures who preached a new vision of society. This privileged youth, riding on the crest of economic security produced by the single-minded effort of their parents after the ruins of a world war, had the time to permit themselves the luxury of enjoying the benefits of the material world and tuning in to the bliss of the spiritual world. The message, as enshrined in a world-wide broadcast by the Beatles at about the same time as man set foot on the Moon, was 'All you need is Love.'

Asked to name the most influential group of people in the sixties, many would identify the Beatles, who broke through in Britain in the early sixties, entered the world stage in the mid-sixties, and left as the seventies dawned. With them along with other figures such as Bob Dylan and the Rolling Stones, was brought a world of colour, sensation, consciousness and concern, using the medium of music in a political and transformative way. So what was it that happened in astrological terms?

It was in fact in the year 1962 that all the visible planets in the solar system – the traditional planets – were for one short time in the sign Aquarius. On 5 February 1962 there was a lunar eclipse at the power point (or avatar degree) of 15 degrees Aquarius. There is a very interesting story connected with this date, documented in Nicholas Campion's invaluable *Book of World Horoscopes*. He relates that in the 1890s a Frenchman called Gabriel Jogand fraudulently predicted the birth of an anti-Christ in the year 1962, as a deliberate ruse to upset Catholics. Subsequently, on this very date, the famous American clairvoyant had a vision of a baby born in the Middle East who would become an 'anti-Christ', leading humanity away from Christianity. She recorded the time, and Nicholas Campion has a horoscope drawn for 5 February at 12.17 GMT in Jerusalem which is supposed to relate to this birth. It is my belief that no single individual will inaugurate the Aquarian Age, but this eclipse must indicate a major transition. Chart 6.4 is for the New Moon. Again it is set for New York, particularly because Pluto rises there at the time of the eclipse. It was after all in this year that there was a major time of pressure for America – the near-nuclear confrontation between Kennedy and Khrushchev over the placing of atomic missiles in Cuba.

In the extraordinarily close conjunction of Jupiter, Venus and retrograde Mercury with the eclipse, we can see the incredibly benevolent influence of Aquarius on the one hand, especially in the form of communication and the media, combined with the iron severity of the close Saturn–Mars conjunction. Note how the dispositor of

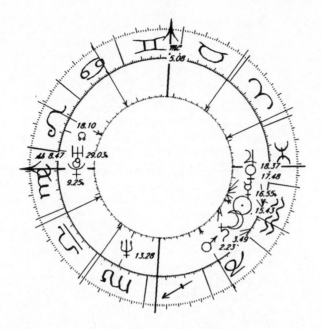

Chart 6.4: Aquarian Eclipse, 5 Feb. 1962, 00.10 GMT, New York.

Aquarius – Uranus – is placed at 29 degrees Leo – on Regulus, the King's Star. Political events notwithstanding, this unusual astronomical event foreshadowed an extraordinary change in the tone of life on Earth in the sixties, with a veritable explosion of new culture based on the vision of the melting together of Eastern and Western culture. This decade was an island of inspiration in the long process of transition – a foretaste of Aquarius.

Engines of Change

If the Aquarian experience can be timed to begin in the year 2020, the beginning of the end of Pisces was certainly in the year 1781. The discovery of Uranus in this year was made possible because of the application of the telescope. This made it possible for the mind of man to reach out

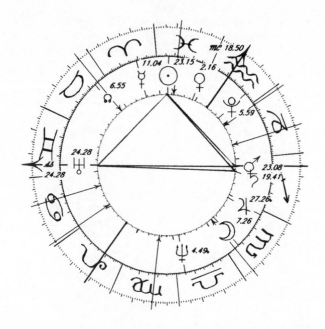

Chart 6.5: Dawn of Uranus, 13 Mar. 1781, 10.09 GMT, Bath

into areas of outer space never before explored. As man expands into outer space he liberates equally vast areas of inner space. In fact it is the sensory system and mind of man which creates the illusion of inner and outer. Chart 6.5 is the horoscope for the dawning of Uranus on the consciousness of man. It is not the actual moment of discovery of Uranus, but the moment Uranus rose over the Eastern horizon over Bath on the day Herschel observed it in his telescope.

This is a remarkable chart, very strongly representing the explosive and revolutionary nature of Uranus, symbolically in opposition to Saturn on the one hand, and Mars on the other. The discovery of Uranus at 24 degrees Gemini sensitises this point as a power point of change, and indicates that communication and travel will be areas of subsequent dramatic change. The as yet undiscovered planets of Pluto and Neptune lie in close trine – also in air signs. With the Uranus–Mars opposition and Moon–Pluto square, this is a violent chart, heralding a violent period in European history, as well as the beginning of the industrial era and the role of the machine in the history of Man.

Marshall McCluhan – American media expert – points out (in *Understanding Media*, Routledge & Kegan Paul) that machines are simply extensions of the sensory system and the mind of man. Just as man exerts a powerful influence on the machine, the machine exerts a powerful influence on man. A rifle, for example, is an extension of the spear, which is an extension of the fist, which is an expression of our anger or fear. But possession of rifles on a mass scale alters consciousness. Print technology is an extension of the mouth and spoken word, yet comes to exert an influence in its own right on the thinking processes of man. The linear construction of sentences in print technology is paralleled by production line techniques which dominated industrial thinking in the Newtonian era (but will not do in the coming robot electronic era of the air mutation). The sequential logic of printed sentences comes to dominate the way our minds work and our whole view of time, especially the way we divide time into 'before' and 'after'. However, in the instant electric environment of the twentieth century, sequential logic is replaced by instantaneous awareness. Our growing familiarity with computer and word-processing techniques – which make possible the wholesale and immediate movement of blocks of information – will be paralleled by a hitherto unseen mind expansion as the human brain is freed from unnecessary information storage and can be utilised more creatively.

As the mind of man reached such a stage of refinement that it was able to discover Uranus, then the magic and power of Uranus made itself felt on the mind of man. One year after its discovery – in 1782 – the Montgolfier brothers finished the construction of their hot-air balloon, which took flight in 1783. For the first time in history the air element had been mastered. Today, at any one moment, hundreds of thousands of people from different lands and cultures are being transported at inconceivable speeds through the skies by the Jumbo jets of the late twentieth century.

Also in the year 1782 James Watt invented the rotary steam engine which very rapidly transformed the industry of the time. Steam had existed since man had harnessed fire, but it was only in the latter stages of the eighteenth century that man could harness the expansive power of steam under compression. And it could only be used because refinements in the iron industry made it possible to bore cylinders accurately. And these cylinders only worked effectively because new technological developments made it possible to create effective seals. As mastery of matter is achieved, technological progress becomes possible. With technological progress, the consciousness of the masses expands. With control of the air and (explosive) gases, the Aquarian Age is inaugurated.

The harnessing of the new technology, synchronistic with the discovery of Uranus, led to the industrial revolution. As men and women left the land to enter the rapidly expanding cities, people began to congregate *en masse* – a basically new historical development. As these masses were driven to earn their living serving the city machines they organised themselves and became aware of their rights. Profound political thinkers like Thomas Paine (who wrote *The Rights of Man* enshrining the principles of Aquarius) formulated basic human rights which became the foundation of the revolutionary constitutions of both America and France. The American constitution states explicitly that the individual is possessed of certain incontestable rights, including the right to be free – and happy! Truly a revolutionary idea after the slavery and serfdom of the past. The influence of revolutionary writers in the late eighteenth century was magnified by new cheap printing methods, so that ideas could be disseminated to everybody – not just the chosen few.

Serfdom was abolished throughout Europe. Before this time people were actually *owned* by the landed gentry and could not move about freely. Now they were at liberty to sell their labour – they were free, though slaves to capital. In France in 1789 the spirit of the new age was so strong that the nobles themselves voted themselves out of power. They placed their own heads on the chopping block, and with the execution of Louis XVI (execution of the king – Leo – elevation of the Paris 'Commune' – Aquarius) the old political order was unequivocally ended. France, intoxicated by the Uranian spirit, declared an end to the old calendar and started a new millennium at the Year One, with new months – Frugtidore, Thermidore, etc. – based on the signs of the zodiac! (This lasted only a few years.) And on the new currency of revolutionary France the motto of the Aquarian Age is printed: 'Liberté, Egalité, Fraternité' – freedom, equality and brotherhood.

Napoleon was a man of his time, of relatively humble birth, who was successful because he understood the democratic forces of the new age, and was idolised by his men. He saw his European campaigns as wars of liberation, and his democratic reorganisation of the army made it possible for natural talent to emerge in contrast to principles of birth and privilege which rendered the forces of his opponents inefficient. It was natural that England, Prussia and Austria joined forces to defeat Napolean – he represented the downfall of the aristocratic structure they stood for.

On the technological front, steam engines soon combined with the wheel, in new systems of mass transport, which exploded previous concepts of speed, noise and pollution. For the human senses of the eighteenth and nineteenth centuries the steam locomotive represented everything that was foreign to their experience – and heralded the mad rush and deafening noise of the modern city today. As the higher octave of Mercury, Uranus exponentially expanded communication potentials, leading to the development of the telegraph, transoceanic undersea cables, the telephone and ultimately to man's dominance of the airwaves through radio and television.

All these things and more have a direct association with the planet Uranus. Practising astrologers will be able to confirm these properties of Uranus in their study of mundane and personal astrological influences. We know that this planet rules revolution and freedom, invention and inspiration, speed and – not least – explosions. This is not just an idea, or a useful metaphor; Uranus is *manifest* in these things, and our experience of all these things is a baptism in the energies and vibration of Uranus.

In understanding the outer planets as the very forces which engineer the transition from Pisces to Aquarius, it is necessary to understand the synchronicity of outer discovery and inner transformation. This can scarcely be better illustrated as far as Uranus is concerned than by the explosion of the Space Shuttle *Challenger* in 1986. Never have so many people simultaneously witnessed so large an explosion. It could be described as the largest explosion in history to date.

This explosion happened at the exact time the spaceship *Voyager* flew past the planet Uranus. This was the scene at NASA, as described by a reporter for *National Geographic*:

> Tuesday, January 28. As Voyager scientists are preparing to sum up the mission to the press, the space shuttle *Challenger* explodes. Those clustered in JPL's press centre share a horrible irony. On one monitor we watch replay after replay of seven lives evaporating over the Atlantic, while on an adjacent TV screen we see the latest triumphant pictures from Uranus.

To know Uranus is to know the explosive power of the sudden and unpredictable.

Sensory Seduction

The discovery of Uranus heralded an explosive mental expansion which led to a new revolutionary spirit. Europe was in turmoil and torn apart by bloody violence. The new freedom for serfs led also to a life of exploitation in the cities. The price of change was high. It is a general characteristic of the Aquarian transition that the human race is dragged almost unwillingly into the future by the technology it creates. We protect ourselves from change by nostalgic longing after the past, and we view the environment around us as something alien and unwanted, an accident for which we are not responsible. We shut out thousands of sensory inputs every day which carry the information of Aquarius. These inputs are alien and unpleasant – we block out the totalitarian hum of our electric world, and this blockage creates dis-ease in us.

With the discovery of Neptune in 1846 the highest spiritual potential of the Piscean Age was accessed. The plight of the masses led to a series of surprisingly non-violent social revolutions in European cities, as workers strove to establish minimum standards of safety, welfare and pay in factories. The books of Charles Dickens reflected the new spirit of social concern that began to affect politics. The first hospitals were created, and anaesthetics developed. (Thus it was in 1846 that the first recorded use of ether took place – creating an altered reality state, and some time later Queen Victoria herself used chloroform during childbirth.) Social reforms at this time foreshadowed the later creation of the welfare state – a truly Neptunian institution. By giving financial support to those people who are out of work, they are spared the great suffering of poverty and material loss. However, anyone who has experienced welfare can also testify to its fantastic undermining effect (Neptune = dissolution) – we have all heard about the family of five who receive more money in supplementary benefits than if the father were to go out to work! Chart 6.6 is the horoscope for the dawning of Neptune prior to its discovery over Berlin later that day. This chart shows that Neptune was discovered when it was in exact conjunction with Saturn at 25 degrees Aquarius, sensitising this degree for social change. It is an interesting fact that the Moon is in Scorpio conjuncting either the North or South nodes at the time of the discovery of all three outer planets, apparently symbolising their transformative powers on the world population. Saturn represents here a strong grounding of Neptune's energies to effect social change (Aquarius). The emphasis in Virgo suggests that it is primarily working conditions that are the centre for the social ideals of this conjunction.

In 1848 the Communist Manifesto was published by Marx and Engels. Communism is a direct expression of Neptunian logic, spawned by concern at the suffering of the masses. (It has also been clearly documented how the Communist world resonates to the Saturn–Neptune conjunction – from the Russian Revolution of 1917, to the death of Stalin in 1953 and indeed the upheavals in Cuba, Russia, Eastern Europe and China in 1989.) In the first page of the Communist manifesto the Neptunian view of reality is clearly expressed. By changing the structure of the social and political environment, the consciousness of the people will likewise be transformed. This view was a

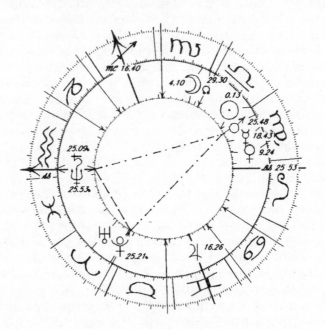

Chart 6.6: Dawn of Neptune, 23 Sept. 1846, 16.00 GMT, Berlin.

natural consequence of the Newtonian mechanical world-view which saw things in terms of cause and effect. By changing the outer environment, the inner environment would follow suit. This sounds good, but is philosophic-ally erroneous. Outer reality and inner consciousness ripen synchronistically in a process of maturing and growth; imposing ideology on unripe consciousness leads to dis-aster. This was the first great illusion of the nineteenth-century Neptune.

I am tempted to suggest that the next great illusion was Darwin's theory of evolution put forward in his revolutionary book *On the Origin of the Species by Natural Selection* in 1859. This suggested that man was the physical result of a process of mutation and refinement (Neptunian principles) in an evolutionary system which saw man as a descendant of the apes, in a long line of mutation and development since the first single-celled microbes which swam about in the primordial soup of pre-history. The impact of this thesis on the Christian tradition at least matched the impact of Marx on the Capitalist tradition, because it directly contradicted the biblical story of the creation of man by God. It also led to a general belief in the doctrine of the survival of the fittest – a godsend for capitalist theory.

Where Uranus transforms mental consciousness, Nep-tune reaches the parts which other planets cannot reach – the inner sense of touch, and the inner landscape of fantasy. It was in the same year as Neptune's discovery that Edward Lear wrote his *Book of Nonsense*! This was also the dawning of the era of the Impressionists. Painters like Renoir, Gauguin, Van Gogh, Cezanne and Monet started to paint their inner reactions to what they saw, so that art became for the first time more than just a pictorial representation of the visual. Neptune accesses the subtle experience of inner touch – the awareness of emotional impact stimulated by outer experience.

The first photographs were taken at this time – with far-reaching consequences. For the first time it became possible to capture reality in an instantaneous process, and store it. The ability to take pictures of 'reality' meant that reality could be repeated and manipulated. Now it was possible to be larger than life! The photographic image led inexorably to the dream machine of Hollywood which created fantasy worlds and recreated history. At the beginning of the twentieth century the cinema became a place of refuge and escape for the downtrodden worker, who could exchange the hard reality of the factory for the dreamworld of stars, riches and happy endings.

Later, film was harnessed in the interests of capitalism as a subtle assault on our inner senses through advertising, stimulating the materialistic drives of the earth mutation. Only in this Neptunian world could it be claimed that 'Coke is the real thing.' Maybe it is. Coca Cola brings the world of luxury to the simplest African or Indian village, and its logo is to be seen in the most unlikely places – from Moscow to the smallest Pacific island.

Before we express our disgust at yet another example of capitalist exploitation, it is well to remember that the African villager wants it this way – Coca Cola is a passport to the world of luxury and pleasure he knows is there, and as such is a levelling factor. Both the rich and poor drink coke and are united thereby. Advertising has a number of creative side-effects. Market forces and advertising costs force the TV advert to minimise its time and maximise its effect, leading to a sharpening of our awareness of the present and a corresponding sophistication of our perceptions. Advertising cleverly exploits the deadly human sin of greed, harnessing this energy to defeat the deadly sin of sloth, so that people unite as co-producers of the transition to Aquarius.

On a spiritual level, the consequence of our colonial expansion into the Third World led to the further undermining of the power of the Church through the influence of other religions. West met East, and wise men of the East introduced concepts of karma and reincarnation to the Western mind. Spiritual movements sprang up in Europe – from the theosophists of the late nineteenth century to the myriad of movements of today. These influences have had a more powerful influence on the youth of the late twentieth century than the traditional Christian philosophy which dominated the last age. As an extra measure to complete the dissolution of the rigid Western mind, drugs permeated in from the East, from the opium which released the imagination of Coleridge and enslaved many of his generation, through the softer hallucinogens of marijuana and LSD, to the heroin, crack and cocaine which undermine the fabric of society today.

Uranus and Neptune joined hands to revolutionise and make pliable human consciousness. Inventions (Uranus) led to a new experience of reality (Neptune). Thus the telephone transformed our experience of time and space. We can now talk to someone in Australia as if they were in the same room as us. This warps the old view of reality and introduces an awareness of relativity. It can be quicker to get a message to someone in Australia than to someone next door. The TV news brings world events into our living space, so that they become the property of each and every individual. So, when Neil Armstrong hops happily on the Moon, watched by hundreds of millions of people simultaneously, one smile breaks out on the Human Face in one precious moment. Mass inner touch. When the Beatles release their new single 'All you need is Love' for the first time in a live worldwide broadcast, what a profound effect it must create in the psyche of the human race!

Neptune unites the world emotionally.

Death and Resurrection

In 1930, precisely one Uranus cycle after the discovery of Neptune in 1846, Pluto was located in the farthest reaches of the solar system. The discovery of Pluto was made possible by the technology associated with Neptune – it was located through the use of a photographic plate. Chart 6.7 is for the dawning of Pluto over Arizona on the day of its discovery.

Chart 6.7: Dawn of Pluto, 18 Feb. 1930, 21.44 GMT, Flagstaff, Arizona

Again we can see the Moon on the nodal axis in Scorpio with the theme of the grounding of cosmic transformative energies. Pluto was discovered at 17°46′ Cancer, a degree which has subsequently been shown to be sensitive. The American astrologer Mark Lerner points out for example that the atomic explosions over Hiroshima and Nagasaki in 1945 happened when Saturn conjuncted this degree.

Since the 1940s Pluto and Neptune have made a sextile to each other, and because of the eccentricity of Pluto's orbit – where it actually enters the orbit of Neptune from 1978 to 1999 – their speed is at this time approximately equal, and the sextile continues into the next century. Their influence is therefore profoundly interlinked in this period. Neptune is said to rule oil, which lubricates Uranian technology, and is the raw material for the contained explosions in present-day combustion engines.

It is from oil that plastic is manufactured, and plastic is Pluto made manifest in matter.

In the unrefined high-energy technology of the twentieth century, oil is burned in motors and even to heat houses. This is the folly of our age. Oil is too precious to burn, because in its form as plastic it will enable the Earth to preserve natural resources and prevent the rape of Nature. Plastic *is* unnatural, and evokes in us immediate alienation, wonder and even disgust. We cherish our mahogany and pine furniture, and despise our plastic products, but plastic is democratic and levels humanity as a necessary transition to the Age of Equality. The quality of plastic defies explanation, its touch defies description, its sound is a sound all of its own. The very molecular structure of plastic is weird and locked in. Most plastics do not break down, they litter the wayside for hundreds of years. Plastic defies disintegration and death; it is not living, not organic.

Without plastic there would be no electronics, no miniaturisation and no transformation of today's political system through the cheap products plastic makes available – products so cheap that they are made to be thrown away when empty. Plastic is taking over like a creeping invasion from another galaxy, appealing to our anxiety and fear of death. In the supermarket, cling-film covers all products for sale, reassuring us that no invisible microbes and germs are there from other human hands to threaten us. Thus plastic adds to our alienation from nature and our fellow humans, as an invisible barrier of touch.

With the discovery of Pluto vast new areas of the solar system were seen to be under the gravitational influence of our Sun. Corresponding areas of inner space were discovered in the human psyche – space filled with hitherto unknown gods and demons. To map this inner space pioneers of psychoanalysis like Freud, Jung and Reich, came into the forefront of the medical world. Here Pluto represents that store of repressed experience which in the form of psychological complexes poisons our present-day behaviour. These complexes are fed by continuous suppression of natural drives because of fear and guilt. In this connection the perversion of the force of sexuality was shown by Freud to be a major factor in personality disorders, and later Reich showed how the experience of the orgasm was a cathartic process which liberated blockage and healed disorder (Wilhelm Reich, *The Function of the Orgasm*). Sexuality was rescued from the forgotten corners of Christian prudishness to come into the forefront of the human psyche and make us whole.

On the international arena demons of destruction were also released. Germany, smarting under the ridiculous humiliation imposed on it by England and France after the First World War, and totally bankrupted, spawned the demoniacal forces of Fascism. As a medium for the fears and frustrations of the German population, Hitler channelled their demons against the Jews. He foresaw a thousand-year Reich dominated by racially 'pure' Aryans with the Germans as the 'master' race (Pluto has associations with the master–slave relationship). This concern with heritage, absolute purity and race is typical of Pluto's connection with roots, clinical cleanliness and power.

The psychologist Wilhelm Reich found in his consultations that patients often associated sexuality with Jews, who featured strongly in their dreams and fantasies. At the same time Jews were despised because of their financial power and their prominence in industry. By channelling German humiliation against the Jews, Hitler was able to key into the destructive powers and passions of Pluto connected with sexuality and 'other people's resources'. Six million Jews died in Nazi extermination camps – an unparalleled destruction of human life. Yet from the ashes of Auschwitz, and the guilt of Europe, a new Jewish state was to arise on the foundations of the old. After 2000 years of wanderings, Jews were able to return to their roots in Israel. Pluto brought death, but also rebirth.

With the splitting of the atom in the twenties, Einstein's theory of relativity was confirmed in practice, and the way was paved for the creation of the atom bomb. No single invention has had such a profound effect on the mind of man. With the explosions over Hiroshima and Nagasaki in August 1945, the world-view was transformed overnight. Japan too rose from the ashes of Plutonian destruction to become a dominant economic power, but from that point world nations were in a state of shock. Just as Neptune harnessed Venusian materialism as a transformative factor, Pluto harnesses the terrors of Mars. For the first time the human race became aware of its vulnerability – now the key to the destruction of man lay in the hand of man, not, apparently, in the hand of God.

Since 1945 the fate of the world has hung in the balance. The effect of Pluto is often to evoke terror. Yet other more positive effects are in direct proportion to its negative effects. Fear and angst (Pluto) is the motivating force of peace in these days. Humans are aware of the Earth as one global unit. In Pluto and the Bomb is embodied the threat of global destruction, yet this destructive power did not arise accidentally. The missiles in France, England, Russia, the United States, India, China, Pakistan, Israel and South Africa, aimed at world capitals are the symbol of the aggression and 'virility' of male government. They are the symbol of collective anger and fear. As such all of us who allow anger to rage within are responsible for this collective manifestation of the power of Mars. If we want to change it, we must change ourselves. Cleverly then, Pluto harnesses the deadly sin of anger in the interests of peace.

Aquarius is the Age of Man, of equality on all levels. 'Man' here means both men and women, yet women have been the victims of discrimination and subjugation during the Christian era, and have perhaps embodied more than men the spirit of sacrifice and suffering of the Piscean Age. In many ways this situation was a result of biological factors – pregnancy definitely slowed women down in life or death situations, so that physically at least, men were endowed with the potential for both protection and domination. This biological imbalance is no longer a decisive factor. In the first half of this century it was not unheard of for women to have ten or more babies. Sexual urges ensured the survival of the species here! In China today it is frowned on to have more than *one* child! In the Western world the emancipation of women has meant that the birth rate has fallen so dramatically that the net population is actually decreasing!

This control over biological factors has been effected by the birth control revolution. Effective condoms, and the use of the pill have prevented fertilisation taking place. The coil and the abortion have resulted in millions of minor murders – beings sacrificed on the altar of Pisces in the name of Pluto. The liberation of the female body from the tyranny of pregnancy has led to an explosion of sexual consciousness. Pluto liberates here the deadly sin of Lust, and lust does service for Pluto and Neptune in the advertising industry. Sex sells, and sex motivates, and it is useful to harness these energies. However, the fact is that in the past sex was sin for a great many people. Now it is no longer a sin – though until a cure for Aids is discovered it may be a health risk.

For women, the ability to prevent pregnancy has meant that they can claim power and equality on the same footing as men, and with the passage of both Pluto and Uranus through Libra in the seventies, the sign of partnership, the women's liberation movement ripped through inequalities both in marriage and the career leaving the traditional man nursing a wounded ego. For the transition from Pisces to Aquarius to take place, sexual equality is essential.

To talk about Pluto, and the life areas it touches, is to set feelings on the boil. Pollution, plastic, Nazism, the Bomb, sex and abortion are subjects charged with our own inner anxieties. Dispassionate discussion is almost impossible – our objective faculties are totally bypassed. There are certain universal characteristics of this planet. One is that its effect is out of all proportion to its size. The first atom bomb was the size of a car battery inside its metal casing, yet could destroy a whole city. To make this release of energy possible it was necessary to create matter in its most intense form – enriched uranium or plutonium. (A

fine choice of names for these most dense of elements! The
French intercontinental rocket is called Pluton!) To create
matter so dense took the finest minds in the scientific
world, and enormous economic resources. Pluto is like a
black hole which absorbs tremendous human resources –
and, in the atomic programme, vast amounts of the tax-
payer's money. This fanatical and single-minded pursuit
of costly goals to assuage fear is typical of Pluto.

At first glance it appears that Pluto's effects, as in the
atom bomb, give far more energy out than was originally
put in. But this is not the case. Pluto simply accesses
energy that has been stored away, and in the atom bomb
it is the energy that originally went into creating matter
at the beginning of time which is released. In the human
psyche it is the energy originally invested in the neurosis
which when liberated transforms the individual. The
same principle can be seen in the computer. A computer
program for generating horoscopes for example appears
to save hours of time for the practising astrologer. Yet
the computer simply accesses the stored-up work of the
programmer (Pluto and the 8th house = other people's
resources) who has spent many months feeding the
computer with information. Computers make the mental
powers of experts available to the common man.

Another characteristic of Pluto is the feature of exponential growth. In a chain reaction for example, one
atom releases several neutrons, which split more atoms,
etc. Computers expand exponentially in their memory
capacity – from 16K to 32K to 64K, etc. Viruses, discovered
in the wake of Pluto, also expand exponentially – computer
viruses too. In the sixties there was a profound fear that
the population was expanding exponentially – and it
was. The important thing about exponential growth, as
a market dynamic made possible by the use of plastic and
electronics, is that products become cheaper and cheaper,
smaller and smaller and more and more effective. This
dynamic spells the end of the days of privilege. The
miniaturisation process brings the material world closer
to the functions of the cellular world, so that the division

between mind and matter is forcibly brought to an end – this is a polarity which will not exist in Aquarian consciousness.

The discovery of Pluto in 1930 heralded the advent of raw power and destruction and it became clear that the human race could eliminate itself. We all live under the 'Nuclear Umbrella' today which 'protects' us from the hard rain of nuclear fall-out. Yet death has always been an inevitable factor of living, and consciousness of death inspires man to live life more intensely and more urgently. The Bomb reminds us that we are alive! Awareness of nuclear power leads to a sense of world responsibility and unity because of the need to take action to eliminate the consequences of human weakness – we become aware of the finite nature of the world's resources, of the consequences of pollution, of the futility of aggression.

The principle of Pluto is crisis leading to rebirth, and it is the human reaction to the negative consequences symbolised by Pluto which lead to resurrection of the planet. The legacy of Pluto is global consciousness.

Pluto's demons are within us. They hide themselves behind our blockages. To flush these demons out means that we have to observe ourselves when we react in an extreme way; it is exactly that issue which we *absolutely* refuse to discuss, or that area where *no* compromise is possible, those times when we are flushed with ideological righteousness, that the Pluto throws aside its invisible cloak. If we embrace this demon, which feeds on our deepest fears, it will be transformed and become our faithful servant.

Waking to Aquarius

As the digital alarm beeps, and we sleepily stumble into the bathroom, let us take a pause before we flush the toilet. Today we are going to wake up to Aquarius. So before we flush we can consider that the modern toilet is a first childhood introduction to Pluto – a sterile world in which 99 per cent of all known germs have been annihilated. This first disappearance of our waste products sets the general tone for later adult life when nobody takes responsibility for their waste. It just disappears, doesn't it?

Listen now, there is a hum. This background noise did not exist just fifty years ago – now it is omnipresent. Did you leave the computer on? Or is it just the refrigerator, which you never turn off? As you open its door to get the milk, note the magical environment within – the transformation of fire (electric current) into ice (Scorpio). After breakfast you may set your robot household in motion: dishwasher, clothes washer, security system (the more you own, the more anxiety you have – Taurus– Scorpio). On the way to work, the streets are awash with traffic noise. In the combustion engine of the car, explosions produce power through sudden expansion of gas (Uranus), and these explosions are muffled through a variety of exhaust styles which produce an orchestra of different sounds which grow in intensity, and then fade away as the cars rush past. Pluto is made manifest through the exhaust, and traffic noise is the signature of Pluto. It is the muffled sound, the subdued sound, which is Pluto – thus the overt roar of the jet plane overhead is Uranus's statement of existence.

You will not feel this, but the air is full of information – radio waves and microwaves channelling a network of minds exchanging a myriad of messages. Under your feet are rushing channels of water, sewage and gas, and a tangle of wire and optic cables entering and uniting every abode like a collective nervous and lymphatic system. On billboards and in neon above the hanging heads of people rushing to work entangled in their thoughts and worries, advertising companies preach the message of capitalism in a totalitarian visual bombardment.

Perhaps you work in the city tax department. As you enter the office illuminated by an array of humming fluorescent tubes you settle down at your desk, switch on your computer and merge with the collective mind.

At your fingertips is basic information about every single member of the nation's population, stored in a central computer – information also accessed by insurance companies, the police, banks and young computer hackers. With a few commands you summon this information laboriously programmed in over the years, and it appears instantaneously. Also from the screen invisible rays emerge, entering and leaving your body and the building, part of the growing accumulation of background radiation which now permeates all our lives. In an economic community which has almost eliminated money, you can follow the plastic transactions of the tax-evader under investigation for the day; where, when and how much he spends – on petrol, in the theatre, in the city's restaurants.

The reader can take comfort however. This same totalitarian web of information will also be available to every individual – the future will bring total access, and freedom of information will be the sepulchre that guarantees individual human rights.

In the office you effortlessly duplicate necessary information on your copying machine. Perhaps you recall the carbon paper of the past and the laborious process of mechanical reproduction that required secretaries involved in repetitious work. A Swiss philosopher once remarked 'Repetition has the smell of death' – but now that burden is shouldered by the electronic brain and steel sinews of the machine – both in the office and the factory.

After a hard day's work you return home to relax in front of the TV, a plastic object placed at the focal point of the furniture in your living room – the shrine of the New Age. As you switch on for the News, you merge with 50 million minds, in a collective groan at the latest strikes, indignation at the latest act of terrorism, smile at the newscaster's joke. A TV company representative rings you and you tell him what programme you watch. Your opinions are duly noted and the TV ratings go up or down. This *is* the dictatorship of the masses as prophesied by Lenin.

In the alchemy of the smoking city and its mighty roar, through the incessant broadcasts on the air, on the collective backs of a suffering humanity, a transformation is taking place. This transformation is using matter to transform spirit. If we look at the symbols of the three outer planets, ♅ ♆ ♇ we can see that they are all based on the cross of matter. The transition to Aquarius happens in the material world, through the material world – it is not effected by the arrival of a new saviour (except Christ incarnate in matter), or through a spiritual élite or through a new religion, but by the simultaneous development of consciousness and technology. The material world is the playground of Uranus, Neptune and Pluto, and in the Aquarian Age people *will* play, not suffer. Of course, most world religions are based on an awareness of the human condition as one of suffering, with Hinduism and Buddhism aimed at liberation of the human soul from the wheel of suffering. But with the transition from Pisces to Aquarius it is the degree of suffering which changes. In Aquarius there is no crucifixion. For the migrating human soul it may indeed have been advantageous to incarnate during the Piscean Age, and obtain purification through suffering.

With the transition from the Mutable Cross of Pisces to the Fixed Cross of Aquarius, it is the air trine which comes to dominate over the water trine, and the two polarities of Aquarius–Leo and Taurus–Scorpio which replace Virgo–Pisces and Gemini–Sagittarius (see Figure 6.4). Through Leo the integrity of the self will be exalted, as people will have a duty to 'find themselves' in contrast to losing themselves in the Piscean Age. The Leo principle is also the principle of fun, entertainment and enjoyment. We can already see how important this is for the modern individual, who, freed from the yoke of suffering by the machine, searches for ways to spend leisure time. This leads to a whole industry of entertainment and pleasure, tourism and mass sports events which lead in turn to rapid and dramatic global union.

Through Taurus, we are steeped in matter and indulgence. Indulgence and ownership have become part of basic human rights, for better or for worse – we are all members of the consumer society. Our desire to possess, a need expanded and fed by the advertising industry to consume the goods that modern production

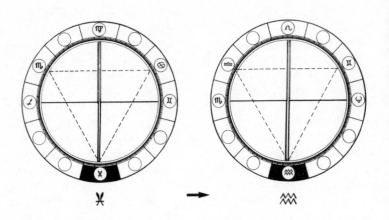

Fig. 6.4 The transition from the Piscean Age to the Aquarian Age

Mutable Grand Cross	*Fixed Grand Cross*
Grand Trine in water	*Grand Trine in air*
Suffering (saved)	Social freedom / mass tyranny
Disintegration (oneness)	Global consciousness
Communism / capitalism	Integration
God / the devil	Paradox
Male / female polarity	Indulgence
Instability	Brotherhood
Repression (Sacrifice)	Global conspiracy / power
Confusion (vision)	Self-assurance (satisfaction)
Spiritual retreat	Mental clarity

methods make possible, would seem ludicrous to the mind of the previous era and offensive to Christian morality. Yet through ownership we come under the sway of matter which transforms and refines our senses. Possessions bring liberation from the yoke of household slavery, experience of new consciousness states (through the Hi-Fi for example), mobility and leisure – but not, of course, peace of mind!

Through Scorpio we integrate the power of sexuality to enrich our pleasure in relationship. The Aquarian age will see a celebration of eroticism. Research into the nature of death through hypnosis and regression brings a new intimacy; and for many death loses its sting because of the influences of the doctrines of karma and reincarnation. New sciences of the mind banish the shadows of the Unconscious – shadows which housed the devils and demons of a previous age. Ultimately the principle of Scorpio will lead to an electronic alchemy which will make all material resources universally available to everybody.

And through Aquarius we will feel global unity – a brotherhood/sisterhood of men and women of all creeds and races. We will be united by freedom of travel and information through a technology so simple and cheap that it will be available to every individual. The only sin in the electric playground of Aquarius is the sin of isolation and separateness. Suffering will be antisocial, and the forces of society will be geared to eliminate it. Aquarius will be a relatively straightforward age, an age of power and intensity. The everyday experience will be so intense in energy that we today could not stand its relentlessness. Aquarius is not for weak souls. Aquarius brings the establishment of *individual* consciousness in contrast to the isolation and loss of identity in higher divinity associated with Pisces. Polarity and dichotomy will dissolve leaving the unity of the ever-present moment.

Whereas the cross was the symbol of power in Pisces, symbolising the crucifixion of Christ in matter, the pentangle will be the symbol of power in Aquarius. It is important to realise that the pentagle has quite different associations to those of the cross – when inverted it is the symbol of satanic forces, whilst when standing on two points it shows man celebrating being in a triumphant stance.

In the Pentagon of the United States is housed the nerve centre of the American military colossus as a symbol of power in the Western world. In the Communist symbolism of Russia and China, the five-pointed star symbolises their power and influence. The pentangle does conjure up a sense of foreboding in many circumstances today. Yet the number 5 also shows the highest potential of human creativity – just as quintile aspects do in the horoscope. The quintile is said to make possible an expression of human individuality and personal style – it embodies a kind of artificiality – and this quality harmonises with a certain sense of artificiality in the Aquarian Age (man-made).

Musicians of the sixties were well aware of this satanic quality of the age, and the five members of the Rolling Stones felt it was time for us to integrate Lucifer, the fallen angel. In songs like 'Their Satanic Majesties' Request' and 'Sympathy for the Devil' they argued the case for reintegrating Satan into consciousness. The reader may think that the idea of satanic energies is going too far, but these energies are all around us. Newspaper editors would once have been burned at the stake for the pictures of nude bodies which they exhibit today, doctors at abortion clinics would have been executed, people who remarry would have been excommunicated. Gluttony, Lust, Sloth, Rage, Envy, Greed and Pride are all alive and well today. More than that they have been collectivised and harnessed as the main transformative factors of the twentieth century! Rage is collectivised under the nuclear umbrella, gluttony and envy in the consumer society, Sloth in our growing leisure time, Pride in the inalienable rights of the individual, Lust in the borderline pornography of many aspects of the media.

The seven deadly sins magnified collectively are outer projections of inner states. If they bother us in the outside world, then we must conquer them within. But these sins are actually the tools of the outer planets in the subtle transition to Aquarius. It is through our weaknesses that we are transformed. We cannot know what Aquarius will bring – true to the nature of its ruling planet, it is a surprise. If we look back over the Age of Pisces we see it as an age split between opposite extremes. With the dawning of Aquarius, the primordial contradiction between Good and Evil will be resolved. The demons within have been released, and they have been welcomed. In our modern lives we experience a new quality, a celebration of desire, a worship of the senses – new colours, new smells, new music, new tastes. Our senses are saturated by a host of pleasures that just two centuries ago would have been abhorred as the work of the devil.

It is the senses that have become vehicles for carrying us over the threshold into a new Age; we cannot yet pierce the veil that hides the future, but we can open our senses to what is happening around us now, instead of blocking them. In the New Age, sin and suffering play only a minor role. But it was sin and the suffering of man for his fellow man that set the tone for the last age – in a sacrifice duplicated by every person in that age – a sacrifice that makes possible the New Age which is about to dawn.